POLICY STUDIES IN EMPLOYMENT AND WELFARE NUMBER 35

General Editor: Sar A. Levitan

UNDERSTANDING THE SERVICE ECONOMY
EMPLOYMENT, PRODUCTIVITY, LOCATION

Thomas M. Stanback, Jr.

with a Foreword by Eli Ginzberg

The Johns Hopkins University Press, Baltimore and London

Manufactured in the United States of America

The Johns Hopkins University Press, Baltimore, Maryland 21218
The Johns Hopkins Press Ltd., London

Library of Congress Catalog Number 79–2372

ISBN 0–8018–2249–1

Library of Congress Cataloging in Publication data
will be found on the last printed page of this book.

The material in this publication was prepared under contract number USDL 21-36-76-18 from the Employment and Training Administration, U.S. Department of Labor, under the authority of Title III, Part B of the Comprehensive Employment and Training Act of 1973. Researchers undertaking such projects under government sponsorship are encouraged to express freely their professional judgment. Therefore, points of view and opinions stated in this document do not necessarily represent the official position or policy of the Department of Labor. Reproduction by the U.S. government in whole or in part is permitted for any purpose.

Contents

Tables

Foreword

Modern economics is a graveyard of concepts that have captured the imagination of professionals and public alike but, with the passage of time, have turned out to have little or no validity. A roll call would include the "theory of stagnation" so popular in the 1930s; the belief in the 1960s that economists knew how to "fine tune" the economy; the widespread conviction of Europeans that they had found the key to "full employment"; the enamorment of the neo-Keynesians with the virtues of "fiscal policy"; and the equal enthusiasm with which their opponents looked to "monetary policy" to solve all problems. And one could go on to list fluctuating exchange rates, monopolistic competition, the benefits (or the defects) of minimum wage legislation, and many more.

The shift of modern economics from goods to services, captured by Daniel Bell's phrase "the post-industrial revolution," is one more illustration of concepts that join center stage without the honing and quantification required to assess their validity. People believe that they know what they mean when they say that our economy has tilted heavily in the direction of service output. This monograph by Thomas Stanback, Jr., was written for the explicit purpose of reviewing what we *really* know about the service economy and what are some of the important implications that can be extracted from such a reassessment.

In addressing this subject, Professor Stanback picks up a theme that has run through the work of the Conservation of Human

Resources Project for more than a decade, as the following paragraphs help to make clear.

In 1965, Dale Hiestand, Beatrice Reubens, and I, reviewing the post–World War II economy of the United States—*The Pluralistic Economy* (McGraw-Hill)—were impressed with the major growth of the not-for-profit sector which governments at all levels dominated. Their differentially rapid growth reflected on the one hand the substantial growth of the defense and space economies; on the other it revealed the striking expansion of public services, particularly in the fields of education, health care, and urban amenities.

At about the same time, 1966, Harry I. Greenfield published his pioneering analysis of *Manpower and the Growth of Producer Services* (Columbia University Press) in which he called attention to the rapid growth of services purchased to facilitate the operation of business enterprises, large, medium, and small. For reasons of efficiency and economy many businesses found it preferable to buy a wide range of services—accounting, computer, legal, management consulting, communications—from specialized organizations rather than to provide them in-house for themselves.

In 1970, Stanback and Richard Knight published their important study of *The Metropolitan Economy* (Columbia University Press) in which they presented a typology of urban places distinguished by their underlying economic structures. In this effort they noted the declining importance of exclusively manufacturing cities such as Pittsburgh, Detroit, and Cincinnati in favor of mixed, nodal, and health-educational and recreational urban complexes, all of which were distinguished in greater or lesser degree by large service components.

Shortly thereafter, in 1973, Richard Knight pushed this approach one step further in his *Employment Expansion and Metropolitan Trade* (Praeger) in which he emphasized through the ingenious use of the extant data the extent to which different urban centers were exporting "services," both business and consumer services, which exports helped to compensate for the loss of exports in goods that characterized most of the older manufacturing centers.

The radical shift in demographic trends that became more clearly visible after the slowdown in the economy's growth after 1969, combined with taxpayer resistance to increased spendings for education, health, and urban services, was a sharp reminder that the earlier presumption of the continued rapid growth of services was not foreordained. Moreover, we had been impressed by Victor Fuchs's work in which he moved against the conventional wisdom by insisting that it made little sense to lump public utilities and communications in the same category as other services because of their heavy dependence on fixed capital and further pointed out that in terms of the value of output (not employment) the figures did not substantiate the commonly held view of a differentially rapid growth of services.

Since the Conservation Project's recent focus has been, and will continue to be, on urban economic development with a special focus on employment, it was essential that the staff gain more understanding of the transformations that were occurring on the service front. This is the task that Stanback addresses in the present work.

What are some of his findings and what bearing do they have for current policies? As a first step toward clarification, Stanback suggests that three types of services be differentiated: consumer, producer, and public. Clearly, such a differentiation is not ironclad. Many firms (legal, accounting) produce both consumer and producer services. And the line between these two categories and public services is not fixed. Refuse collection, for example, usually a public service, is in some communities carried out by the private sector. Nevertheless, the sources of demand for services differ to the extent that they are primarily consumer-, producer-, or public-based, which justifies this simple differentiation.

More important by far is Stanback's statistical analysis, which points up beyond challenge that there has not been any significant tilting of the economy in terms of the value of output from goods to services. His analysis reaffirms that employment has grown very much faster in service than in the goods-producing sector. It is Stanback's considered view, and one that I share, that market forces (elasticity of demand) would preclude an indefinite expansion of services unless the consumer were to lose all taste for additional goods. This does not appear to be the case in an economy in which families seek two cars, two homes, multiple TVs. Stanback also finds merit in his colleague Dale Hiestand's observation of the way the increased demand for services often calls forth the production of new goods from refrigerators to stereos.

In addition to warning against oversimplistic formulations and uncritical projections of trends, Stanback concludes that the goods-producing sector of the U.S. economy is in no danger of early eclipse. The more interesting question that he raises is whether, with so large a part of the total population now employed in services—about three out of five—we stand on the threshold of a major drive to rationalize the production of many of these services. Stanback reminds us that such a likelihood is not pure speculation considering the significant gains that have occurred in many service sectors where personnel has been cut back, from supermarkets to gas stations, from clerical operations to housekeeping. He is unable to pin down the extent to which managerial initiatives and technological developments will lead to the accelerated replacement of labor with capital in the service areas that currently are dependent on large work forces.

Drawing on his special expertise, Stanback introduces a critical new dimension to the conventional analysis of the service economy, that of location. He raises and discusses the distribution of different types of service employment by different types of work places and further introduces considerations of the range and quality of the jobs that are encompassed within the service sector. To take the last point first: in contrast to common belief, he finds that a high proportion of all service jobs are at the lower end of the wage structure. With respect to location, Stanback finds that while residentiary services for consumers tend to follow population relocations, business services and to a lesser degree public services (universities, major medical centers, government offices) are more unevenly distributed. This means that some urban centers such as New York City or Atlanta are much better positioned with respect to job creation and income generation because of the export potential of their services than communities that are relatively underdeveloped with respect to business and public services.

On the basis of these lines of analysis, Stanback raises three policy issues in his concluding chapter. The first is focused on the outlook for major technological changes affecting the level and trend in white collar employment. Without repeating the snatches of evidence that Stanback has identified, suffice it to say that he believes that because of the large numbers now employed in such activities and the dynamic nature of the new technology the setting is favorable for a strong and continuing employer effort to move toward increased use of technology so that the office of tomorrow will have more machines and fewer people. Stanback is by no means certain that this will happen—and the events of the last twenty years speak against a rapid transformation—but at the least the issue is worth keeping under close scrutiny.

With the president (and the Congress) increasingly committed to reducing the government's share in the gross national product and speeding the day when the federal budget will be balanced and with the mood of Proposition 13 gaining adherents from the West Coast to the East Coast, there does not appear to be any large-scale expansion of public sector services in the wings, a conclusion reinforced by the easing of demographic pressures. Here is a second growth area that is beginning to level off, if not decline.

The third development the author raises is the likelihood of a sizable expansion in small-scale enterprise. There is some suggestion in the recent data that self-employment is on the increase. It may well prove to be a source of employment growth for both consumer and producer services. But we will need more time, more data, and more analyses before any firm conclusions can be drawn about developments on this front. All one can say for now is that self-employment should be kept under surveillance.

There are two ways to read Stanback's analysis if one's major concern is with the future of job creation in the U.S. economy. The pessimistic approach would be to give dominant weight to his findings that the powerful forces stimulating service employment expansion during the past decades have weakened perceptively, considering the potential leveling off of public sector expenditures and the serious threat that looms ahead from advances in office automation.

But there is an alternative explanation. The downstream potential for the continued erosion of manufacturing jobs (and possibly jobs in mining) may be exaggerated. The growth of service employment places a premium on capital investment aimed at containing this trend. Moreover, the changing international economic picture with the less expensive dollar should likewise stimulate our manufacturing sales abroad. There is a reasonable chance that if service employment slows up, manufacturing may fill some if not all of the gap. There is one other factor: not today nor tomorrow, but by the late 1980s and beyond, the inflow of new workers into the labor force should, in the absence of an uncontrolled flow of illegal immigrants, help to ease the balance between job applicants and jobs.

But no matter what the future will reveal, Stanback has helped us to monitor the years ahead by increasing our understanding of the service economy.

Columbia University
Eli Ginzberg, Director
Conservation of Human Resources

Acknowledgments

My thanks are due to a number of my colleagues at the Conservation of Human Resources Project, Columbia University, who have assisted me in the preparation of this monograph. Eli Ginzberg, Charles Brecher, Marcia Freedman, Dean Morse, and Thierry Noyelle gave valuable critical advice. Tom Wong compiled the data and made the necessary computations, and Joanne Koeller cheerfully and carefully typed and retyped the manuscript.

Understanding the Service Economy

1

Introduction

One of the most widely heralded developments of the postwar years has been the relatively rapid growth of employment in those activities we commonly designate as services. In 1929, services accounted for 40 percent of total employment, in 1947, shortly after the end of World War II, for 46 percent, and by 1976, for roughly 61 percent.[1]

Though generally recognized, this dramatic increase in employment has not for the most part been critically examined and is largely misunderstood.[2] Contributing to this misunderstanding are at least three major failures of perception:

1. The failure to distinguish between services output and services employment, which has led to the mistaken view that we are moving into a new era in which demand for services is increasing rapidly while demand for goods is leveling off.

2. The failure to distinguish among major types of services— consumer, producer, and public sector—which has obstructed intelligent discussion of trends in service growth.

3. The failure to view the growth of services in relation to the processes of urbanization, or, more particularly, to distinguish between those services a metropolis "exports" and those it provides for residents within its "local sector." This failure has brought with it a lack of understanding of the extent to which the economic vitality of cities rests on their ability to compete as ser-

vice centers within a national and international system of metropolitan places.

This monograph is aimed at clarifying these perceptual failures and in the process providing some insight into the transformation that is taking place in the nature of employment by answering a variety of questions: (1) Who is getting the rapidly expanding service jobs? (2) What kind of wages/income attach to them? (3) What information can be extracted about the continuing growth of such jobs with regard to occupational trends? (4) What are the implications for a U.S. economy in which service employment continues to grow but under conditions of at least some unfavorable differential between productivity gains in services and goods?

The study does not undertake to break new ground as a statistical investigation of demand relationships or to provide new measures of output or productivity trends. Rather, its approach is largely to reexamine materials relating to service sector structure and growth under the four major headings of demand, productivity, employment, and urbanization, focusing primarily on the manpower and urban implications of the growth of services.

General Conclusions

Four general conclusions flow out of the analysis:

1. There are strong linkages between goods and services arising out of complementarities of demand. In consumption these complementarities stem largely from joint use, in particular, the need to distribute and maintain goods. In production they are increasingly the result of the growing complexity of the managerial task, which creates new requirements for outside expertise, and the growing usefulness of producer service firms as they become increasingly specialized and add new functions. In the public sector they stem from the heavy goods content of many services (for example, health, military) and from the fact that government is to a large extent servicing (and regulating) a complex industrial society.

Coupled with this complementarity is the ever-present possibility of substitution of goods for services when cost and price trends in services are unfavorable. Such substitution restricts the development of significant tendencies of the economy to veer sharply away from the production of goods and toward the production of services.

All this is consistent with the general observation of Victor Fuchs that, when output is measured in constant dollars, there has been very little shift from goods to services since 1961 (see table 1).[3]

Table 1. Shares of Employment* and GNP by Sector, Selected Years, 1948 to 1976.

	1948	1961	1976
Employment			
Agriculture	10.8	6.9	4.2
Industry†	43.2	38.6	35.1
Services	46.0	54.5	60.7
GNP (current dollar)			
Agriculture	9.8	4.2	3.1
Industry†	46.8	45.0	41.2
Services	43.9	50.8	55.7
GNP (1972 dollar)			
Agriculture	5.8	4.3	2.9
Industry†	43.0	40.7	40.7
Services	51.3	55.0	56.3

Source: Victor R. Fuchs, *The Service Industries and U.S. Economic Growth Since World War II*, NBER Working Paper, No. 211 (Stanford, Calif.: National Bureau of Economic Research, Inc., 1977), p.46.

*Full-time equivalent persons engaged.

†Industry includes mining, construction, manufacturing, transportation, communications, and public utilities.

2. There are new forces at work that promise significant productivity gains in services. They arise in large measure from new managerial approaches to the organization of service firms and institutions, coupled with applications of new technology. These gains should be seen in perspective, however. In spite of major obstacles to accurate measurement of output in most services, there would seem to be little doubt that significant differentials continue to exist between productivity in goods and services taken as aggregates and that differentials in rates of productivity improvement will not soon be erased.

For services that are produced in the private sector, such differentials will for the most part cause no great difficulty. Buyers and sellers will adjust through a combination of substituting that which is cheaper for that which is dearer, modifying goods and services, or, when necessary, simply accepting higher cost and price. In the public sector, however, response is likely to be both insensitive and irrational. For a complex society that looks to the public sector to provide a great variety of services not ordinarily responsive to the signals of the marketplace, new approaches to management leading to greater overall effectiveness become crucial.

3. Contrary to much that has been said, the service work force is not, on average, better paid or more highly skilled than the non-service work force. Although in the top reaches of the distribution of service jobs one finds a substantial number of highly paid, skilled professionals and executives of large service firms, the service work force is hierarchically structured in terms of earnings, with the low-paying jobs comprising a disproportionate share of the total. In contrast to nonservice employment, it is characterized by a larger proportion of workers at the lower end of the earnings scale, by a higher proportion of women and minority workers, by higher percentages of part-time employment, and by fewer structural and institutional arrangements that enhance job security. Moreover, the evidence does not point to a generalized trend toward an upward redistribution of service jobs. Growth in services is strongly associated with increasing employment of women, and female earning levels are being upgraded to some extent. But, in general, employment expansion is occurring at all levels of the occupational and income scales.

Since service employment expansion appears to be the major source of growth in jobs within the economy, the sex, occupational, and earnings characteristics of new jobs opening up in the services are of strategic importance.

4. Examination of employment in metropolitan areas within the framework of urban economic theory helps to make clear how occupational and skill mixes vary from place to place and sheds light on both manpower and urban development policy. As employment in goods production shifts, cities must seek to offset employment deficits. In part, additional employment has occurred through growth in local, residentially oriented services that have expanded everywhere. But in services that are "exported," expan-

sion has been selective. Metropolitan places in regions favored by growth and those that have in the past become specialized as service centers have fared best. But the analysis is complicated by possibilities of geographical shifts in services as well as goods. How central cities will fare in competition with suburban and nonmetropolitan places is subject to a variety of social and demographic factors, at least some of which are favorable and can provide a basis upon which aggressive new public sector development policies may be grounded.

A Technical Note:
The Distinction between Goods and Services

Implicit in all that has been said is the assumption that the concept of a group of economic activities labeled "services" represents a valid category for analysis. Clearly, activities commonly described as services vary widely. Some, such as legal and accounting services, are heavily labor intensive. Others, such as communications and utilities, are heavily capital intensive. Some service firms are small, others are very large. Yet there is an important distinction to be made between most goods and most services. Production of "goods" results in a material product that is typically storable and transportable. Production of "services" results in an output that is not storable and usually requires direct interaction with the customer. This distinction means that goods can usually be produced more readily than services under conditions that take advantage of standardized output and economies of scale. In general, this has resulted in differences both in location and in the ability of firms to employ capital-intensive modes of production. Goods tend to be produced by firms employing a considerable amount of equipment. Goods can be—and increasingly are—produced away from cities. Services are typically less standardized, and the firms that produce them tend to be located close to the markets they serve, often in congested urban areas.

How, then, are we to define services in such a way as to exclude activities that are most "goodslike" in such fundamental characteristics as tendency to utilize heavily capital-intensive and large-scale modes of production? The solution employed here is to

5

restrict the definition of services to include only wholesale and retail trade, FIRE (finance, insurance, and real estate), general government, professional, personal, business, and repair services.[4] Transportation, communication, and public utilities—activities often considered as services but typically capital intensive and large in scale—are included along with mining, construction, and manufacturing in a single sector, "industry." Services along with the two goods sectors, industry and agriculture, constitute the total economy (see table 1).

It is important to emphasize that in the above discussion and in the analysis to follow services are defined as outputs of firms or other organizations and do not include servicelike functions performed within nonservice organizations. For example, the counsel provided by a legal firm to a client is considered to be a service, but the work performed by the legal staff within a manufacturing corporation is not.

Rising employment in servicelike functions performed within nonservice organizations is by no means an unimportant part of the transformation that is taking place within the American economy as a result of both a changing bill of goods produced and changes in the way we get things done. This is illustrated by the fact that during the two decades 1957–77 the percentage of total employment in manufacturing accounted for by nonproduction workers increased from 23 to 29 percent, indicating a sharp rise in the number of jobs relating to record keeping, analysis, management, finance, sales research, and other functions necessary in the production and distribution of goods.

Nevertheless, the study of services as outputs warrants our principal attention. By far the largest share of employment growth has been occurring in private and public sector service establishments, and such data as are available relating to occupations (Chapter 4) indicate that most of the shifts toward servicelike work are taking place within the service sector. Moreover, there seems to be a significant tendency for service-producing organizations to take over servicelike functions as new needs develop and as such functions become of greater importance.

2

The Demand for Services

Demand analysis stands as the initial task in determining what forces have been at work in the economy in recent decades and whether such forces are rapidly propelling us toward an economy involved principally in the production of services rather than goods. The following discussion treats the factors that influence expenditures for consumers services, producer services, and public sector services as well as certain constraints that may work to limit significant shifts from goods to services. The chapter concludes with an examination of how costs and the possibilities for substitutions combine with the rise of new needs for services to determine the mix of goods and services within the total economy.

Consumer Expenditures

The view that the American society is rapidly moving into an era in which consumption is largely oriented toward services is by no means an accurate one. Consumption expenditures for services did rise at rates well in excess of growth of disposable personal income during the fifties (Table 2), but during most of the period thereafter growth has been roughly comparable, whether measured in current or constant dollars. For the relatively prosperous years from 1960 to 1973, increases in services expenditures simply kept pace with growth in disposable income when comparisons are made in constant dollar terms. Increases in current dollar terms were slightly higher, however. In more recent years, with the slowing down in national product increases in service expenditures have somewhat outpaced rises in disposable income.

Taking the period since 1950 as a whole, the share of consumer expenditures accounted for by services has grown sharply, but it is by no means evident that this share will rise rapidly or even significantly in the years ahead. It is important to observe that for most of the period since 1960 expenditures for durable goods have risen more rapidly than for services even though price increases in services have been greater. From 1960 to 1973 expenditures for durables increased at an annual rate of 8.5 percent in current dollars while services grew at a rate of 7.9 percent. During the period of sharp inflation since 1973, expenditures for services have risen more rapidly, but this has been largely due to differential rates of price increase. The share of consumer expenditures accounted for by durables declined slightly when measured in current dollars but increased in constant dollar terms.

This tendency for consumer expenditures for durable goods to grow at rates roughly comparable to expenditures for services is not necessarily as surprising a finding as at first it might appear to be. A colleague of mine is fond of saying, "We Americans tend to take our services out in goods." By this he means that Americans are strongly disposed to equip themselves heavily and fully for each new activity, especially for leisure activities. The dramatic increase in popularity of tennis, for example, has given rise to a great spurt in demand not only for tennis racquets, balls, nets, and court maintenance equipment but for a variety of tennis apparel and luggage. The increasing interest in rock, country, and classical music has produced sharp rises in the demand for stereo sets and records, and the widespread popularity of boating has resulted in an increase in boat ownership. Even in the area of home maintenance, the strong trend toward "do-it-yourself" has led to substantial increases in sales of hardware and maintenance supplies.

But perhaps a broader and more useful generalization is simply that there is a high degree of complementarity between consumer goods, especially durables, and many services. The increased

Table 2. Annual Rates of Increase in Consumer Expenditures, Price Levels, and Shares, by Major Types, Selected Periods and Years, 1950 to 1977.

	Rates of change, consumer expenditures and price levels*			Shares, consumer expenditures			
	1950-60	1960-73	1973-77†	1950	1960	1973	1977†
In current dollars							
Total goods	4.2	6.8	9.6	67.2	59.8	56.5	54.5
Durable goods	3.4 (1.5)	8.5 (1.6)	9.8 (6.4)	(16.0)	(13.3)	(15.3)	(14.8)
Nondurable goods	4.4 (1.8)	6.3 (3.1)	9.5 (7.5)	(51.2)	(46.5)	(41.2)	(39.7)
Services	7.6 (3.7)	7.9 (3.4)	11.8 (7.8)	32.8	40.2	43.5	45.5
Total expenditures	5.4	7.3	10.6	100.0	100.0	100.0	100.0
Disposable income	5.5	7.6	9.8				
In 1972 dollars							
Total goods	2.4	3.9	2.1	60.7	56.6	56.2	54.8
Durable goods	1.9	6.7	3.1	(12.8)	(11.6)	(15.9)	(16.1)
Nondurable goods	2.5	3.1	1.6	(47.9)	(46.0)	(40.3)	(38.7)
Services	3.8	4.4	3.7	39.3	42.4	43.8	45.2
Total expenditures	3.0	4.2	2.8	100.0	100.0	100.0	100.0
Disposable income	3.0	4.4	2.1				

Source: *The Economic Report of the President* (Washington, D.C.: U.S. Government Printing Office, 1978), pp. 258, 260, 272, 283.

*Rates of change in price levels in parenthesis.

†All expenditures and price data for 1977 are preliminary.

consumption of automobiles is associated with increased mainten-ance and routine fuel servicing. Increased travel involves con-sumption of motel and restaurant services and of transportation-oriented goods. Increased participation in sports and recreation creates a demand for new equipment as well as for services. The family home requires a combination of housing structure, house-hold furnishings, and supplies along with a variety of services. Perhaps most important, the purchase of consumer goods requires a matching component of retail services.

Not all of the demand for services by consumers is complemen-tary to the demand for goods. Some services, identified in Table 3 as medical, personal business, personal care, higher education, and foreign travel services, are, for the most part, not complemen-tary. In 1973 these accounted for 14.5 percent of total consumers expenditures, in comparison to services identified as usually complementary (household operations, auto services, other rec-reational items) which constituted 12 percent. Two categories, shelter expenditures, 14.4 percent (which is not principally for services as conventionally conceived but rather is a combination of the imputed value of rentals on owned homes plus tenant payments for rent), and "all other" (5 percent) were not classified. Although these classifications are rough it would appear that services may be regarded as being complementarily related to goods to an impor-tant degree, perhaps by as much as 45 percent, for consumer service expenditures as we ordinarily speak of them.

There are important new trends in expenditures for certain consumers services, of course, and the future will probably see still further reallocations of expenditures among specific services. Demographic shifts have exerted a powerful force in the past and may be expected to play a major role in the years ahead. Just as the earlier postwar period saw increases in demand for the services of the obstetrician and the pediatrician and for special educational services for the young, the years ahead may be expected to show sharp rises in the need for the services of those who specialize in geriatric medicine, retirement and nursing institutions, and adult education. There has been a marked increase in the popularity of dining out (both in fast food and conventional restaurants),

Table 3. Personal Consumption Expenditures by Types,
Shares, and Annual Rates of Growth, Indexes of Price Increase, 1960 to 1973.

Total Expenditures	100.0	7.2	4.4	1.64
Food	18.0	5.7	1.9	3.00
Apparel	8.7	7.5	4.3	1.74
Home	27.6	7.4	5.0	1.48
Shelter†	14.4	7.3	4.7	1.55
Household operations†	5.9	6.9	4.6	1.50
Furniture	1.4	7.1	4.0	1.78
Appliances	1.6	7.6	7.7	0.99
Miscellaneous Household Durables	2.3	8.9	6.9	1.29
House furnishings	1.2	9.7	7.1	1.37
Household supplies	0.8	5.6	4.0	1.40
Automobile	12.4	7.5	5.7	1.32
Cars	6.0	8.3	7.4	1.12
Tires, tubes, accessories	0.9	9.3	7.9	1.18
Gasoline and oil	3.5	6.7	4.7	1.43
Auto services†	2.0	6.4	2.7	2.37
Personal care products and services	9.2	9.0	4.9	1.84
Drugs	1.1	6.9	6.6	1.04
Toiletries	1.0	7.7	6.3	1.22
Medical services†	6.5	10.2	4.9	2.08
Personal care services†	0.6	5.1	1.6	3.19
Luxury and nonessential	13.3	7.5	4.9	1.53
TV, radios, records	1.6	10.8	11.7	0.92
Boats, sport equipment	0.9	9.7	8.8	1.10
Alcoholic beverages	2.7	5.7	3.9	1.46
Higher education†	0.8	11.7	5.8	2.02
Foreign travel†	0.9	9.3	5.8	1.60
Tobacco	1.7	5.3	1.6	3.31
Jewelry, watches	0.6	6.8	6.1	1.12
Other recreational items	4.1	8.0	4.3	1.86
Other	10.7	7.2	5.6	1.29
Personal business services†	5.7	8.9	4.6	1.94
All other†	5.0	5.6	6.8	0.82

Source: Adapted from Fabian Linden, "Affluence in the Go–Go Era," *Conference Board Record* 12 (May 1975): 21.
*Annual.
†Entirely or largely services.

influenced at least in part by the increase in households with working wives and the increase in households headed by unattached individuals. These trends, however, do not negate the point that for much consumption there is an essentially complementary relationship that should bring about a more or less matching stream of goods and services in the years ahead as in the past.

Linder's Theory of Consumption

Considerable light is shed on the nature of consumer demand for services in Stefan B. Linder's *The Harried Leisure Class*, published in 1970.[1] Linder is concerned with restating the theory of consumer behavior in such a way as to make consumption subject not only to the constraint of income (the budget constraint) but also to the constraint of time. He emphasizes that, whereas real income per capita is continuously rising through increased productivity, time is constant and can only be reallocated. The consumer (increasingly the family unit with the wife employed either part or full time) divides time between work, consumption, and maintenance activities. Since increases in productivity raise the availability of consumer goods more than the availability of consumption time, there is an increasing consumption intensity in the use of time. What follows is not only the development of a culture in which life is more hurried (harried) but one in which consumption patterns are rearranged to favor activities that are relatively goods-intensive (the older, time-intensive activities become in the economist's language "inferior" activities). Moreover, goods require time not only for consumption but for maintenance, and an increasing ownership of goods causes an increasing demand upon time for maintenance. This, too, increases the intensity of time utilization.

Linder's treatment of services performed outside the home deals largely with maintenance of consumer goods. In an age of specialization, consumers may purchase maintenance services in lieu of providing them personally, but they do so subject to cost constraints that have advanced steadily. Productivity gains in services have been smaller than in goods, partly because there has been less room for mechanization. Thus the cost of such services has risen relative to the cost of goods.

In our society, rising costs of maintenance may be dealt with by producing throwaway or shorter-lived products (because maintenance increases with product life) or by accepting lower standards of quality in maintenance services. The tendency toward the latter may be endemic within the system. In both the private and public sectors the quality of services appears to be deteriorating: auto repairs are more expensive and less effective, mail deliveries are slower, streets are dirtier, and so on. All these stand simply as a reflection of an ongoing process by which society economizes on relatively costly services.

Finally, Linder finds no evidence that the percentage of time devoted to work is declining.[2] He admits that, theoretically, worktime might decrease even though the intensity of utilization of nonwork time continues to rise (that is, we could conceivably work fewer hours, thereby freeing up time, while continuing to become more harried in our so-called leisure time as our level of consumption rises disproportionately); but there is no evidence that such has occurred. Properly adjusted, the data show no tendency for the number of desired working hours to decline since World War II (though there was a trend toward reduction in working hours prewar). Moreover, given the apparent high income elasticity of demand for new and novel goods, he sees little reason to expect workers to deliberately sacrifice earnings by shortening their work weeks.

The above brief review of Linder's analysis provides a basis for a number of observations of major importance in any discussion of the demand for services. The first is simply that the fairly rigid constraints on time available for consumption along with an increasing cheapness of goods relative to services would account, at least in part, for the strong goods orientation in consumption patterns noted earlier.

The second is that the outputs of goods and services are likely to rise together (the complementarity discussed above) because goods frequently require maintenance and because consumption patterns often involve a combination of goods and services (Linder does not delve into the latter). Nevertheless, to the extent that productivity gains are less rapid in services, resulting in higher costs, the first observation continues to hold: there will be constraints upon expansion of demand for services. These con-

13

straints will occur in a variety of forms involving efforts to substitute goods for services, to economize on the use of services, and to substitute goods-rich for goods-poor patterns of consumption.

The third is that there is reason to question the widely held assumption that leisure time is increasing and that greater amounts of leisure time will bring a greater demand for leisure-related services. If, however, leisure time is not increasing, there will be less reason for the demand for leisure-related services to expand.

A fourth observation flows out of remarks of Linder not yet discussed. In his analysis of tendencies to economize on maintenance services through early replacement of goods, he calls attention to the fact that such an option is not available for the maintenance of our irreplaceable bodies through medical care. He speculates that in order to maintain our bodies—indeed, to extend through health care our consumption capacity over a greater number of years—we may very well increase our demand for health services disproportionately as income rises.[3] In economic terminology, the demand for health services is probably income elastic.

Similarly, expenditures for certain types of education may act to increase earning capacity and thus our total consumption over time. Accordingly, expenditures for technical and professional education may be income elastic. But, given the relative increase in tuition and the increasing scarcity of time, such would not be the case for educational services that only broaden our horizons intellectually and culturally and do not increase our earning capacity.

A fifth observation involves the significance of productivity. Is the assumption regarding lower productivity valid for all or most of the services? If productivity does not rise as rapidly in services as in goods, then the efforts to economize on services described above must follow, for services become progressively more expensive relative to goods. If, however, productivity does rise as rapidly in services, much of the analysis is invalidated. It is for this reason that the question of productivity assumes major significance and is discussed at some length in Chapter 3.

The Implications of Growing Aggregate Demand

During the period from 1950 to 1976, the rise in population and per capita income has been accompanied by an increase in total consumption expenditures of 143 percent measured in constant dollars—an expansion that has been widely diffused throughout the economy. This expansion of consumer markets has led to at least two developments that must be recognized if one is to understand what has taken place in the marketing of consumer services.

The first involves an increased standardization arising out of a shift from a local and regional to a national basis in the merchandising of a number of services. Along with the growth of income and population that has increased market potentials, an increased mobility of the population and a rise in the role of mass communication, especially TV, have acted to reduce sharply regional differences in consumption patterns. The standardization of goods, which is not a new development, has been joined increasingly by a standardization of services. Not only do Americans today dress alike, drive the same makes of cars, equip their homes with the same furnishings and appliances, and eat the same brands of foods, but they dine at identical fast food restaurants, sleep overnight in motels operated by the same motel chains, enjoy the same TV and movie entertainment, read the same national magazines, buy the same insurance, finance their automobiles and appliances through the same credit firms, and charge a variety of purchases with the same credit cards.

The social implications of this increasing uniformity of consumption patterns among different regions may be uncertain, but the economic implications are clear: there have been increasing opportunities for standardization in the delivery of services and for the successful operation of large, multibranched corporations or franchised operations, a subject to be examined at greater length in the discussion of trends in productivity.

The second development involves, paradoxically, an increase in the variety of services. As population and income have grown, it has become economically feasible for an ever greater number of firms to enter the marketplace offering new types of services. In

15

this way, the broader and richer markets of the postwar years have acted to increase the range of consumer choice.

This proliferation of services may well have contributed to a distorted perception of the growth of consumer services. New types of services, particularly new types of retailing, are highly visible. If, as has typically been the case in every community of substantial size, a number of new service outlets appear in quick succession—a pizza parlor, Burger-King restaurant, tennis supply shop, bike shop, cheese store, poodle shearing parlor, unisex barber shop (in addition to the previous barber and beauty shops), and so on—it is easy to conclude that there has been a vast increase in the total share of income spent for services. Yet such a conclusion need not follow. A proliferation of services and of service firms in an expanding market will bring about, as we have noted, a greater range of choice for the consumer, and, most likely, a reallocation of his purchases, but it need not increase the share of his total expenditures for services.

A corollary observation regarding this increasing variety of consumer services is that it does not appear to have reduced the extent to which demand for consumer goods and consumer services is complementary. In part, this is because consumers tend to consume goods and services jointly, as noted above, but in part it is simply because the new proliferation involves retailing. Tennis shops, pet shops, camera shops, bike shops, mountaineering and skiing centers are essentially firms that combine advice and a sharing of interests and experience with the dispensing of goods. Even such operations as ski and tennis centers and marinas rely heavily on consumer purchases of equipment and supplies to generate sufficient sales revenues to permit profitable operation.

The thrust of these observations is once again that there appears to be no significant trend away from goods and toward services in the pattern of consumer expenditures, but rather that the purchases of many goods and services are closely linked.

Producer Services

The input-output tables for the American economy show that more than a fourth (26.7 percent) of all intermediate outputs—

outputs of firms that are purchased by other firms as inputs for further production—are services (table 4). These intermediate services—producer services—are principally wholesaling, FIRE, and a wide-ranging group of "business services" that include advertising, legal, engineering, auditing, consulting, and a variety of lesser services such as telephone answering, janitorial work, and provision of temporary office help.

Table 4. Interindustry Transactions, 1967.

	Intermediate* outputs share	Percent of total† intermediate outputs
Nonservices	54.3	73.3
Primary (agriculture, mining, fisheries)	87.9	11.4
Construction	17.1	2.6
Manufacturing	54.9	49.7
Transportation and Warehousing	60.9	4.7
Communications	55.1	1.8
Utilities	57.3	3.1
Services	37.0	26.7
Wholesale and retail trade	26.0	6.2
Finance, insurance, and real estate	37.7	8.9
Hotels; personal and repair services, exc. auto	22.3	0.7
Business services	83.5	6.9
Auto repair and services	43.9	0.9
Amusements	37.2	0.5
Medical, educational services, and nonprofit organizations	5.5	0.4
Government enterprises	82.3	2.1
Total	48.3	100.0

Source: U.S. Department of Commerce, Survey of Current Business, February 1974, Table 1.
*Share of total output in given industrial classifications.
†Percentage of total intermediate outputs (excluding imports and dummy industries).

The producer services cannot be identified unambiguously by use of standard industrial classifications, however, because at least some firms in virtually every service classification sell to some extent in the intermediate output market. Nevertheless, it is apparent that certain firms are much more heavily engaged as producer service firms than others. For example, in the input-output data, the categories of wholesaling, FIRE, and business services together account for a major share of the intermediate outputs sold by all service firms.

In general, producer services have grown rapidly. Although reliable output data are not available for all service classifications, constant dollar GNP estimates for wholesaling and FIRE show that these classifications grew at rates well above the average for total national product during the quarter century 1950–76. The more detailed employment data indicate that as a group firms that are specialized in the delivery of producer services grew more rapidly than those that retail consumer goods or specialize in providing consumer services.

Factors Influencing Demand for Producer Services

To understand the forces that lie behind such growth we must examine the principal determinants of demand for producer services (that is, why are producer services employed?) and seek out changes within the economy that have acted to increase the importance of these determinants.

Greenfield has enumerated a number of factors that influence an organization to make use of producer services.[4] These factors reduce roughly as follows: (1) The desire to produce at lower cost through "contracting-out," a procedure in which the firm, institution, or government agency turns over to a "contractor" a function—accounting, legal work, transportation, window cleaning—that might have been carried out within the organization itself, but because of scale economies, can be performed more cheaply by an outside firm. (2) The desire to increase the quantity of output by making use of a contractor firm's personnel, which are not needed on a full-time basis, rather than by expanding the basic producing organization. This objective may be coupled, at times, with a further specific objective of maintaining a small and relatively homogeneous work force. (3) The need to tap the expertise of specialists who can keep the firm abreast of new technology, assist in updating the product, minimize risks, and provide guidance with respect to the firm's growth.

In a recent study of advanced corporate services, those producer service firms (such as lawyers, accountants, bankers, and consultants) that deal directly with the large corporate headquarters, Robert Cohen points to a number of additional factors that have acted to increase the importance of the more highly sophisticated and centralized service firms.[5]

The consolidation of smaller firms into larger units has made the management task more complex and increased demand for accounting, financial, consulting, and legal services. The pace of the merger movement has quickened markedly during the past two decades. During the five-year period 1955–59, there were 3,365 mergers and acquisitions compared to 1,424 from 1950 to 1954. In 1960–64, the number rose to 4,366 and again in 1965–70 to 8,213. The pace slackened somewhat from 1970 to 1974, because of the recession and greater difficulty of obtaining finance. Nevertheless, mergers exceeded 5,000, topping all but the immediate preceding period.

Diversification of corporate product lines has made management tasks more complex and has increased demand for specialized corporate services. Whereas trends toward increasing horizontal and vertical integration extend back over many decades, the movement toward acquisition of subsidiaries producing dissimilar products is relatively new. When corporations take over firms in entirely new fields, as in the case of Mobil's acquisition of Montgomery Ward or Philip Morris's assumption of control of Miller Brewing, management is faced with new sets of responsibilities relating to suppliers, production processes, legal issues, financial management, credit demands, and marketing strategies. These conditions force management to rely more heavily than before upon firms that can provide the expertise to permit the new operations to be carried out without an interlude of costly experimentation and mismanagement and can provide a continuous source of counsel and reassessment of policy as the complex conglomerate organization pursues its objectives over time.

The combination of consolidation and diversification has led to increased dependence on financial institutions. In addition, new forms of financing, including greater reliance on debt financing, have given rise to a need for expanded relations with investment and commercial bankers, accountants, and lawyers.

Increased government regulation of the economy has increased the demand for legal and accounting services. For example, recent pension legislation places new requirements upon employers, including submission of all existing and new plans to both the Labor and Treasury Departments.

Expansion into international markets has increased the demand for finance, law, accounting, and consulting services.

Cohen has observed further that advanced corporate service firms have responded to the increasing needs of corporations in a number of ways that have increased their effectiveness and altered their structure. Banks now advise on selection of investments for corporate portfolios as well as simply on matters concerning credit. Accounting firms provide management consulting and corporate evaluations for the financial community in addition to traditional services of audit and tax advice. Law firms provide strategic advice regarding recent and pending legislation as well as defending clients in court. At the same time, new types of advanced service firms have emerged offering counsel relating not only to problems of management but to a variety of technical and scientific matters or engaging in research into an increasing variety of corporate questions, including market potentials and product acceptance.

At least some of the factors that have caused greater demand for advanced corporate services act also to increase the demand of smaller firms for producer services. In particular, this need has arisen in response to increases in government regulation and the increasing complexity of tax laws. Firms of all sizes have frequent need of expert advice relating to union negotiations, pension plans, right-to-work legislation, pollution control, as well as need for accounting expertise for investment tax and accelerated depreciation credits for tax purposes. Moreover, as service firms become increasingly capable of delivering a variety of sophisticated services, smaller businesses increasingly stand to gain by greater reliance on such firms, especially on banks, accountants, lawyers, advertising firms, investment counseling services, and market research firms.

Here increasing market size has played an important role. Data processing firms, accountants, advertising firms, and banks find the potential for sales sufficiently large to offer a variety of services relating to accounts receivable and inventory accounting, investment, financial management, and marketing counsel to medium-sized and small business accounts. Similarly, for a large number of relatively routine services such as janitorial work, office machinery repair, message delivery, and typing, markets have become broad enough to permit firms to set up shop and make themselves available to business customers.

Finally, at least some of the above forces have increased the demand for firms selling business services to the consumer. In recent years we have witnessed the rise of firms offering assistance in preparation of income tax, brokerage houses increasing the variety of services available to the individual investor, banks offering a wider range of investment and loan plans as well as financial counseling, insurance companies increasing the variety of life, auto, home, and other policies and standing ready to analyze the client's special needs. All this is consistent with the observed sharp increase in consumer expenditures for business services noted earlier in the chapter.

The Complementarity between Production and Producer Services

Thus far I have argued that a producer service is employed because the producer finds that certain functions can be handled more effectively and cheaply by shifting them to an independent service organization. Presumably, the service could have been handled by the producing firm (that is, "in-house"). Yet in an important sense the modern capitalistic economy has been made possible by the development of a number of strategic business services or servicelike activities—transportation, distribution, communication, and financial—many of which individual producing firms could not have performed themselves. The opening up of the continent was grounded on a principle of regional specialization of industry and agriculture, made possible by the development of the railway and, subsequently, the highway system, the telegraph and telephone, the modern banking system with its procedures for check clearance and credit extension, the growth and increasing sophistication of modern insurance carriers, and the evolution and increased differentiation among a number of highly effective wholesaling, brokerage, and selling organizations. Thus, to an important extent, the rise of producer service firms has sparked the proliferation and growth of goods-producing firms as well as the other way around.

In the final analysis, the issue is not whether there is a rise in "contracting-out" or of independent service organizations, but whether service functions and production activities are strongly linked. Certainly the history of the modern business economy indicates that they have been and that they will continue to be. A world that increasingly emphasizes the development of expertise is likely to have an increasing need for producer services.

Trends toward In-house Performance of Service Functions

A final issue is whether we are moving toward provision of a greater or lesser share of producer functions by service firms rather than in-house. There is evidence working in both directions. On one hand, major corporations are growing in size and importance. In some cases the firm finds that increasing size makes it feasible to perform a larger share of its functions within the organization (for example, legal functions may be to a greater extent taken over by corporate counsel). On the other, the need for higher levels of expertise coupled with increasing size of the market, which results in lower costs and higher levels of effectiveness for the independent service firm, encourages growth of producer services. This is a matter for further study, although the trends discernible thus far would indicate a strong tendency for the latter set of forces to dominate.

Public Sector Services

Eli Ginzberg has noted that the not-for-profit sector (largely the public sector but also including nonprofit organizations) was responsible directly or indirectly for over a fourth of GNP in 1973, up from 16 percent in 1950, and for just under a third of employment in 1973, compared to roughly a fifth in 1950.[6] A breakdown of purchases of goods and services by general government and nonprofit institutions (table 5) shows that both have enlarged their shares of national employment and of expenditures significantly since 1950 and that, for both, the shares accounted for by direct expenditures are substantially larger than those resulting from purchase from the private sector.

Table 5. Purchases of Goods and Services by General Government and Nonprofit Institutions and Related Employment as Shares of Total, 1950 and 1973.

	Percent of GNP	
	1950	1973
Purchases of goods and services	100.0	100.0
General government	13.3	21.3
Employee compensation	7.3	11.5
Purchases from private sector	6.0	9.9
Nonprofit institutions	2.5	4.9
Employee compensation	1.4	2.8
Purchases from private sector	1.2	2.1
Total direct and indirect purchases	15.8	26.3

	Percent of total employment	
	1950	1970
Employment	100.0	100.0
General government	16.6	24.2
Direct	11.2	15.8
Indirect (private sector)	5.4	8.4
Nonprofit institutions	4.1	7.7
Direct	3.0	5.9
Indirect (private sector)	1.1	1.8
Total direct and indirect employment	20.7	31.9

Source: Dale L. Hiestand, "Recent Trends in the Not-for-Profit Sector," in Research Papers: Sponsored by the Commission on Private Philanthropy and Public Needs, Volume I, History, Trends and Current Magnitudes (Washington, D.C.: U.S. Department of the Treasury, 1977), pp. 333–37.

Public sector services have grown in response to changing demands for improved services, particularly for education, health, and welfare and for such conventional services as police, fire, and sanitation, demands that could not have been met readily, if at all, by the market sector. The result has been an expansion, largely of state and local governments and of nonprofit institutions, particularly colleges, universities, and hospitals. Ginzberg concludes,

23

"Important as the private sector has been in stimulating the growth of the American economy, there is no way to read our recent history except to recognize the strategic part the government and nonprofit institutions have come to play in providing new entrepreneurial structures essential for meeting the new needs and desires of the public."[7]

The variety and importance of changes to which the public sector has been required to respond are most readily illustrated in the areas of educational, health, and urban services. Over the last quarter century the demand for educational services has been influenced by continuous changes in the age structure of our population. The special educational requirements of a series of different age brackets have had to be met in rapid succession as the "baby boom" generation passed from infancy to adulthood. In recent years, the requirements for educational services in the primary and intermediate grades have declined sharply. Similar declines in the need for higher levels of instruction in the years immediately ahead are foreseen.

The rapid increase in total demand for health services has also been influenced by demographic forces, as the older population segment has grown. A heightened awareness of the importance of health services coupled with the appearance of a variety of innovations in funding and institutional arrangements, including third-party payments through private insurance, medicare, and medicaid, have had large employment effects. Finally, new demands for government services have arisen out of needs related to increasing proportions of our population living in urban places, new modes of living, including greater reliance on automotive transportation, and new perceptions of priorities, such as personal safety against crime.

From shortly after World War II until roughly the beginning of the present decade, both absolute and relative government expenditures grew sharply. During these years, the overall growth rate was high and per capita income was rising rapidly. Enjoying a new prosperity displayed by consumption of autos, TVs, new houses, clothes, and the like, the voter accepted easily the need to provide increased health care, education, and social services. Out of a rising

24

income, the citizen gave up annually an ever-increasing flow of tax dollars.

During these years, the growth of employment-intensive public sector services provided a major means for absorbing an expanding labor force, while at the same time agricultural employment was declining and manufacturing employment was growing only slowly. The seventies, however, have brought lower rates of growth of national product and personal income along with inflation and higher unemployment. They have brought also an increasing resistance to further enlargement of government through higher taxes.

Goods-Services Demand Linkages and the Outlook for Public Sector Services

In discussing consumer and producer services, I have emphasized the complementarity that exists between goods and services. To an important degree, complementarity extends also between the rise in output in the private sector (principally in goods production) and the demand for public sector services. Growth in the need for information, regulation, protection (police and fire), pollution and waste control—all related to an expanding industrial society—is the basis for important increases in public sector responsibility, as is the need for enlarged transportation and educational facilities.

In addition, there is a high goods content to the major public sector services. Health, education, and general government institutions have a continuous demand for equipment and supplies, ambulances, trucks and other vehicles, uniforms, books, fuel, and food, and they make major expenditures for facilities. According to a recent estimate, total investment in the very rapid expansion of health manpower from the mid-sixties to the mid-seventies (a large share of which was funded by the public sector) amounted to roughly $20 billion; almost one-fourth went to construction of additional educational facilities.[8]

But these observations do not detract from Ginzberg's insight that the public sector's postwar growth has come largely as a response to needs that could not be met, or at least were not being met, within the private sector. The rapid postwar growth of public sector activities has focused mainly on three general areas: defense, health, and education, of which the latter two are strongly service oriented. The issue to be faced is whether society's needs that require public sector attention will continue to be heavily concentrated in these areas and whether new programs will continue to emphasize service activities.

Although I do not wish to try to predict the future, it is useful to observe current trends and to take account of major unmet needs that might possibly give rise to important new social programs. An initial observation is that education and health services appear to be at a stage beyond which they are not likely to be substantially modified through growth. In the American primary and secondary school system, enrollment has declined from 46.7 million in 1972–73 to 45.2 million in 1976–77, reflecting the aging of the "baby boom" generation. Projections of enrollment in institutions of higher education indicate that attendance will grow at declining rates or will decline after 1977 and that by 1983 the annual rate of change is unlikely to be above 1 percent.[9] While it is likely that education in the future will play at least as important a role as currently in the lives of individual citizens, the demographic basis for rapid expansion no longer exists. In the health field, the situation is somewhat different. A gradually rising percentage of persons over sixty-five years of age will tend to create some new demands on the system; but it is important to recognize that we seem to be entering an era when the capacity to deliver health services will be more than adequate for the job at hand.[10]

As we look around us to determine what new needs are beginning to demand attention, we are struck by the fact that many fall within the areas of goods production: the opening up of new energy sources, the provision of new and different types of housing and the modification of existing housing to conserve energy, the renewal of the decaying inner-city capital infrastructure, the enlarging and modernization of the public transportation system. To the extent that these needs are met, it is likely that the manufacturing and construction industries will be primarily involved, with sponsorship, support, and direction from new public sector structures, and, most likely, with accompanying demands for new services both in the public and private sectors. Although little can be predicted with confidence, in looking to the future there would seem to be no justification for simple extrapolation of trends that have dominated the most recent decades.

The Other Side of Demand: Opportunities for Substitution

Thus far I have emphasized the linkages between demand for goods and services with only occasional reference to the role of cost or of possible substitutions in affecting expenditures for services. Yet a fundamental lesson of economics is that the mix of goods and services utilized in production or consumption is influenced by the prices that must be paid and the opportunities for substitution that are feasible.

Both private sector consumer and producer services compete in the marketplace and face the constraints of competition. In the consumer market, the buyer is aware of unfavorable trends in the relative prices of services and is in a position to respond by economizing on the service in question—substituting goods for services, favoring goods that require less maintenance, and reducing maintenance. In the intermediate market, buyers respond to a rising price of producer services by using less of the service or by performing the service in-house.

In the public sector, however, services are not influenced to the same extent by the economizing process. The voter is not aware of individual price tags on public sector services. Moreover, the influence of particular groups at the polls in determining the quantity or mix of services is not directly correlated with their share of taxes levied. For a variety of reasons, the majority of voters have in the past perceived an increasing need to expand public services (for example, health, police protection, welfare). Yet, ultimately, demand for public services is at least partially responsive to rising costs. As the burden of taxes increases, the taxpayer reacts more strongly and finds a voice through his legislator. Services are curtailed or performed more cheaply and less well; some substitution of goods for services occurs. The process is more indirect, more protracted, and, even in the long run, less sensitive than in the marketplace, but it is, nevertheless, continuously at work.

This analysis does not lead to any firm conclusions as to how far we may expect the public sector to expand or just what mix of public sector services may be expected in the years ahead. It does lead, however, to two general observations. The first is that the role of the public sector will probably continue to be one of complementing (and supplementing) a complex, highly specialized, market-oriented society. The second is that the taxpayer will be responsive, albeit slowly and erratically, to a rising burden of public sector costs. In the end the options available through the legislative process are the same as those available to the purchaser of either consumer or producer services. The service function may be curtailed, it may be supplied by less costly means, or it may be shifted to different institutional arrangements.

3

Productivity

It has been clear since the beginning of this analysis that productivity is a key issue in assessing the role of services in our economy. There is little evidence of a strong, cumulative shift of demand from goods to services. Yet the shift toward greater shares of employment in services is well established. For services, taken as a whole, gains in productivity have failed to match those in nonservice activities; consequently, economic growth has been accompanied by disproportionately large increases in service sector jobs.

This generalized finding gives rise to three major questions: (1) Are there new forces at work that give promise of significant gains in productivity in services in the years ahead? (2) What special problems arise in measuring productivity gains in the services? (3) What are the implications of continued unfavorable differentials in productivity gains in services and of failure to perceive the true productivity levels of services when services are closely linked to goods production?

Forces Influencing Productivity in Services

There are essentially two views of the differential between productivity increases in goods and services. The first sees the trend continuing. This view, implicit in Linder's consumption-time analysis, has been most completely elaborated by William Baumol.[1] In his model of the economy, the result of lower rates of improvement in service productivity is a "cost disease." Wages tend to be set in the goods sector, where workers are rewarded for productivity increases by wage increases that, being roughly proportionate to rates of increase in output, need not bring about significant price increases. But such rates of wage increase tend to "roll out" to the service sector, where they are large relative to rates of productivity increase (and where wages are, typically, a larger share of costs). The result is a continuous rise in unit costs and prices of services.

The impact of lower productivity improvement in services is particularly serious in government—especially in local government—where the demand for services is expanding most rapidly at a time when cities face a variety of problems that are reducing the tax base.[2] Higher public service costs make necessary a reduction of services, bring on higher tax levies, or result in new demands upon already burdened state and federal coffers.

The arts and certain service-rich amenities face another major threat. There is little scope for increased productivity in organizations such as symphony orchestras, opera and theatrical companies, or even gourmet restaurants. Accordingly, these services suffer from high costs and an increasing competitive disadvantage.

The economy *as a whole* is more productive—per capita income is higher because of a rise in *average* output per worker. Consumers could afford a bit more of everything, but the tendency for service costs to rise disproportionately brings a "cost disease" throughout the service sector. The result is a curtailment of services, a deterioration in quality (which, as we have seen, is but another form of economizing), and an increase in tax burdens with costs of public services rising in spite of efforts to keep them in check (for example, the case of New York City, where ceilings on employment have recently been put into force in many departments).

The other view, which finds evidence of a new trend toward more rapid productivity increases in the services, has been set forth by Theodore Leavitt in an article, "Management and the 'Post Industrial' Society."[3] Leavitt holds that the belief that services must be relatively less productive than goods is based on failure to understand the role of management in improving labor productivity. Application of purposeful management practice to the services is increasingly bringing about an "industrialization of service" and a marked improvement in performance.

Leavitt argues that in any economic activity productivity gains come only after the application of managerial direction: "Management consists of the rational assessment of a situation and the systematic development of goals and purposes (what is to be done?); the systematic development of strategies to achieve those goals; the marshalling of the required resources; the rational design, organization, direction, and control of the activities required to attain selected purposes; and finally the motivating and rewarding of people to do the work."[4]

He asserts that the predominant view of the superiority of the goods sector in increasing productivity emphasizes technology and capital to the exclusion of management. But history is replete with examples of major advances that failed to come about with the development of new technology and had to await the initiative and ingenuity of management application or resulted principally from new ways of looking at the job to be done. The advent of Henry Ford's assembly line, for example, was sparked not by new scientific achievement but by his observation of techniques employed by a Sears Roebuck Chicago mail order warehouse in assembling orders for delivery;[5] the supermarket was the result of rearranging the store in such a way as to shift to the customer the task of selecting the merchandise.

Thus, manufacturing's greater success in achieving productivity increases should be seen as the effect of its strong orientation toward the efficient production of results rather than "toward ritual or attendance on others" as in the services. Leavitt writes, "In the manufacturing cognitive mode, the search for improvement seldom focuses on ways to improve personal performance in present tasks, but rather on discovering entirely new ways of performing tasks, or better yet, on actually changing the tasks themselves."[6]

New management methods in reorganizing tasks have brought about improvement of productivity in the services. A classic case is McDonald's restaurants, which have enjoyed spectacular growth.

This organization has succeeded by delivering low-priced, high-quality prepared foods in clean and attractive surroundings. Efficiency is maximized by careful planning of supply arrangements and of layout, by premeasurement of servings, and by careful standardizing of every aspect of the operation from the menu to methods of storage and of food handling, types of equipment and training of personnel, resulting, of course, in a standardized product.[7]

What, then, are we to conclude regarding the outlook for increased productivity in services? At least four major factors work toward increasing efficiency in a variety of service activities. First, productivity increases in services through new managerial methods of the sort discussed by Leavitt are increasingly being observed. Not only may such changes be found in the fast food industry but also in a variety of other activities. We find them, for example, in the hotel and motel industry, where the chores of cleaning and making beds are typically subjected to systematic division of labor, and in government, where new experiments in task definition and budgeting are being initiated.

A second factor contributing to higher productivity is the increasing scale of operation of many service firms, which is associated with the growth of urban markets and with a general tendency for firms and institutions to become national or international in their scope of operations (a development noted in Chapter 2). In a number of instances, new opportunities for application of improved managerial techniques have come through widespread franchising arrangements in which methods of operation as well as the final service output are standardized by the franchising operation, permitting not only new arrangements of work but the application of specialized equipment to at least part of the output. A survey of the Bureau of Domestic Commerce revealed that in 1974 roughly 444,000 establishments were engaged in franchised business with receipts of almost $162 billion.[8]

A third factor is the increased availability of technology appropriate to a variety of service industries. As insightful as Leavitt's observations on the importance of managerial application may be, the fact remains that since the beginning of the industrial revolution scientific and engineering advances have brought about the development of machinery and of new materials more suitable to the improved production and transportation of goods than to raising levels of productivity in the services (with such exceptions as the telephone, the typewriter, the elevator, and a number of highly effective devices in the health services). Only in recent years has a technology become available that is widely applicable to both goods and service firms. This technology, which relates to the modern electronic computer increasingly integrated with telephone, television, and xerography, has demonstrated the capability of significantly increasing output per man hour in activities involving record keeping, communication, or retrieval of information.

Many service industries are now big enough to provide major targets for those who devise new technology and produce the accompanying equipment. ATT, IBM, Xerox, GE, and a large group of new rivals have turned their attention to adapting computer and communications technology to the problems of the retailer, the bank, the hospital, the office, the university, the public school, and virtually every level and branch of government. Their laboratories devise new equipment and new applications while their sales engineers demonstrate to management how work may be rearranged to accommodate the new technology.

Examples of applications of the new technology abound. A recent analysis of service sector trends by the Department of Commerce noted:

Increasingly, the computer is being utilized in a variety of service industries. The introduction of computerized records has reduced manpower requirements and sharply increased productivity in finance, airlines, insurance, and real estate. Computers have revolutionized airline reservation systems and the maintenance of library archives. In the health services industry, computer technology has eliminated endless clerical tasks and is even being used to automate physical examinations. Similarly, recently developed electronic bank teller terminals offer fast deposit, withdrawal, and funds transfer services, reducing long lines in front of tellers' windows. To monitor warehouse inventories, visual display terminals are capable of increasing order-selecting productivity and reducing warehouse operating costs. In

Tacoma, Washington, a computerized court scheduling system saved about 40 percent in police overtime costs during the first 13 months of operation.

In the retail field, a few supermarket chains are testing an automated pricing and checkout system that identifies prices, adds a customer's bill and, at the same time, offers instant inventory control and a method to check results of the store's sales and promotion campaigns.[9]

The fourth factor is more general. Both goods and services output have grown rapidly in the postwar period. For goods, these years were an extension of earlier agricultural and industrial development, and firms raised production levels through the time-honored approach of increasing inputs of capital and labor and improving industrial technology. For the services, however, these were years of unprecedented growth in which the challenge to management was simply to cope with rapidly rising demand. The challenge was answered but largely through expanded employment and at relatively high costs. This was particularly true in handling the vast increase in paper work in offices.

Now, at last, the challenge is changing. The new priority is to rationalize—to do the job at lower cost. This challenge is widely recognized, and the means for substantial increases through work arrangements and applications of computerization and the new technology of "word processing" are at hand.

But it is unlikely that these factors, as important as they may be, will soon close the gap in rates of productivity improvement between goods and services. We cannot fail to note that the success of management in raising productivity in manufacturing continues to be heavily influenced by the very characteristic that, as noted earlier, serves to distinguish goods from services: the opportunity for standardization and large-scale production that allows management to reconceptualize and reorganize operations. The same is true for a number of quasi-service activities that resemble manufacturing in their scale of organization and offer opportunities for standardization of output and adaptation to new technology. In the telephone industry, for example, the introduction of direct dialing along with computerized billing has made possible a vast increase in total volume of telephone and line services with only small increases in employment. A less dramatic but impressive example is found in the airline industry, where computerized reservation and ticketing services have permitted high levels of growth with only relatively modest increases in personnel. Still further advances would seem to be on the horizon.

But similar opportunities for standardization do not hold across a broad spectrum of service activities. The needs to serve each customer individually, to locate so as to attain maximum feasible access to him, and to adapt to his individual needs continue to place restrictions on standardization and scale of operation and thereby to restrict rates of increase in productivity. Moreover, a disproportionately large number of service firms are limited in their scale of operation.[10]

Problems in the Measurement of Productivity

Thus far I have discussed productivity without recognizing that a very basic problem exists in measuring differences in output (and, accordingly, in productivity) between goods and services as well as among the various service activities. How is one to measure the output of a hospital, a university, or a government agency for the year 1978, much less determine how much output has increased over the preceding decade?[11]

The problem lies not only in determining units of measurement of output but also in taking account of changes of quality that in themselves contribute to changes in total output. In health services, advances in knowledge and the development of new drugs, new procedures, and new equipment make it possible to save lives today that would have been lost a decade ago, thereby affecting the total output of health services. Similarly, the increase in number and convenience of services available to consumers, such as customers of banks and insurance companies and vacationers (through a variety of travel agent services, reservation services, and methods of payment), must be regarded as changes both in quality and in volume of output. Likewise, banks, lawyers, and accountants, as noted previously, now offer a greater range of services as well as increasing expertise to their business clientele.

35

In the public sector, a variety of improved services are continuously being made available in such areas as crime detection, meteorology, agricultural research, and pollution control.

Victor Fuchs, who has pioneered in the study of services, has recently noted the following difficulties in measuring productivity:

> One huge caveat must be attached to the finding concerning sector differentials in productivity. As is well known, the methods used to measure "real output" in services frequently fall short of a desirable standard. For instance, until the recent revisions, output in government was simply equated with full-time-equivalent employment. Output per worker never changed, by definition. The revised method is based on employee hours in the various civil service and wage board grades weighted by the 1972 payrolls in these grades. That is, changes in the "quality" of labor measured by changes in the mix of grades are assumed to produce proportional changes in output. Changes in capital stocks or technology continue to be ignored.
>
> Another problem area is banking. Prior to the revisions, output in banking (and other financial intermediaries except life insurance carriers) was indexed by constant dollar deposits. This produced an apparent sharp decline in banking productivity over time as the value of services provided per constant dollar deposits rose. This approach was discarded in the last revision. Now real output in banking is assumed to be proportional to full-time-equivalent employment![12]

But yet another difficulty in measurement of productivity arises out of the linkage of demand for certain services with the demand for the output of other firms or agencies. The problem is simply that the value of the service rests on the value it imparts to the associated activity. Consider the case of producer services. As corporations become larger and more complex and their efficient management increasingly involves reliance on key advanced corporate services, the productivity of such services tends to rise with the significance of the role they play. Thus one cannot speak of the productivity of a highly trained consulting engineer in terms of the number of reports rendered per annum but in terms of the impact of the service rendered upon the overall efficiency of the producing organizations that are his clients, and his productivity may rise as his work becomes more critical. Similarly, productivity (in economic terms) of an educational institution, whether a secondary school or a graduate school of business, must in the final analysis be conceived in terms of its contribution to the efficiency of the economic institutions that are ultimately affected, and the productivity of a fire department or police force rests upon the value of the protection it affords as reflected in the increased efficiency of the city.

Implications of Continued Differentials in Gains in Productivity between Goods and Services

But what is the significance of what has been said above? What difference does it make whether productivity increases as rapidly for services as for goods, whether there are misperceptions regarding the productivity of services, or whether there is a special complementary relationship between certain services and other outputs within the economy?

Implications for the Private Sector

One observation is that in the private sector marketplace the demand linkages that arise out of complementarity tend to reduce the buyer's sensitivity to price changes. Consider the case of automobile ownership. Operation of an automobile requires not only a car, gasoline, oil, replacement tires, batteries, and so on, but maintenance and refueling services. If advances in productivity lag in the service activities, which comprise but a small share of cost of operation, the total costs of operation are not affected greatly in percentage terms, and the total demand for automobile travel is not likely to be curtailed significantly. Thus, for such services, differentials in rates of productivity advances are of no great moment, particularly if the entire bundle of goods and services is being produced under conditions in which overall productivity is rising at about the same rates as those of rival goods and services.

The complementary relationship is, of course, likely to be subject to some modification over time. The substitution principle will be at work even though it may be limited. Thus, in operating automobiles, less expensive services may be substituted for those that are more costly (self-service may replace use of attendants in dispensing gasoline, cars may be redesigned to require less frequent oil change and repairs), and in managing businesses, alternative arrangements (perhaps involving new technology) will be adopted, and pressures to find new structures will develop. Once again, there need be no major shifts away from or toward services.

For such services, and there are many, the marketplace performs as an effective arbiter in directing resources to their most economical use. Discrepancies in rates of productivity as reflected in increases in relative prices are either accepted or met with appropriate adjustment.

Implications for the Public Sector

Where the public sector is involved, however, the problem becomes more serious. If, for example, the quantity of garbage removed per man hour in a city fails to rise in proportion to the wages of sanitation workers as determined by general wage levels, the relative cost of garbage removal rises, and a greater burden is placed on the tax base. The options faced are to find new and cheaper ways to remove garbage, to curtail garbage collection, or to continue garbage collection at a higher total cost.

Clearly, the service demand here is linked to the overall operation of the city's economy, and it is not unlikely that the true productivity of sanitation workers is higher when streets are cleaned thoroughly than when they are cleaned poorly even when measured output per hour is the same. Clean streets are probably a minimum requirement in retaining businesses and residents and permitting the continued economic functioning of the city and the maintenance of its tax base over time. Dirty streets cause the city to become dysfunctional and contribute to the erosion of the tax base. It may well be claimed that the public can afford clean streets if it can afford the city and that it cannot afford dirty streets at all.

But this does not solve the problem. Very likely, the true productivity of the service will not be perceived. More serious yet, the increasing cost of city services, as reflected in higher taxes, simply invites the shift of businesses and residents to other areas, where, for a while at least, costs are lower. Higher costs resulting from perceived, not true, productivity differentials lie at the heart of the problems of cities and of towns everywhere today.

Moreover, the difficulty of placing a value on services output may lead to misallocation of such resources as the public sector can command. The inability to determine the value of parks, recreational programs, or a higher teacher-student ratio in ghetto schools frequently leads to a channeling of funds away from such budget items, although in both long-run economic and quality-of-life terms they may have been far better candidates for retention than the favored alternatives.

Robert Mowitz, in analyzing obstacles to increased productivity in government, has identified five major problems. The first is conceptual. He sees productivity as related to the manner in which *goals* and *objectives* are achieved. Goals he defines as the values of a particular government system; they "are subjective and express preferred states about which there is some concensus ... such as protection of persons and property, and minimized health hazards." Objectives are "those physical states ... which unlike goals, are observable, quantifiable and occur in real time... A targeted infant mortality rate thus would serve as an explicit objective satisfying a health goal."[13]

The second relates to the search for means whereby targeted objectives can be accomplished:

> For example, if the objective is to reduce loss of life and property due to fire, the subsystems include builders, manufacturers of building materials and insurance companies, as well as governmental subsystems in the form of building regulations, inspectors, water systems and fire departments. Analysis of the fire defense system might reveal that installation of smoke detection sensors would do more to reduce the response time of fire departments than relocation of fire houses. If that were the case, then enhancing productivity might be accomplished through a change in insurance premiums thereby providing an incentive for the use of the sensors.[14]

The remaining three problems involve determining how work is to be done, establishing standards of performance, and coordinating the agencies involved. Determining how work is to be done is seen as essentially technological: finding the way of performing work that costs least once objectives have been established and the work necessary to accomplish these objectives has been determined. This is the area on which most work in public sector productivity has been focused. Establishing standards of performance involves what Mowitz calls avoiding "managing in the dark." Although public sector record keeping is often elaborate, the failure to establish objectives means that management information systems typically fail to specify the information required in order to determine whether or not programs are on target and if not where they are missing. The final problem is concerned with coordination. Since public sector activities frequently require joint action by several agencies, the problem of scheduling and coordination makes necessary "some system of program management which will not only pinpoint responsibilities for the coordinating activities on a program basis, but also provide authority to back up the responsibility."[15]

The issue of productivity in the public sector has been discussed at some length because the implications of failure to achieve high productivity are more serious than for the private sector. In the private sector we are willing to leave the problem of raising levels of productivity to individual firms and to allow the customer to make adjustments by choosing among alternatives of goods and services (each with its separate price tag) available in the marketplace. But, as noted in Chapter 2, the response to rising prices in the public sector is less sensitive and more protracted and has been accompanied by widespread dissatisfaction with the high costs of government. If, indeed, the role of the public sector in a complex modern society is to make provision for critical needs that will not otherwise be met, then a new and more effective approach to improving productivity in government stands as a major challenge.

Summary and Conclusions

At the beginning of this chapter, questions were raised relating to the promise of productivity gains in the services, the special problems of measuring productivity, and the implications of continued unfavorable productivity differentials in services relative to goods production.

Three conclusions seem justified:

1. There are indeed new forces at work that promise significant gains in productivity. They arise in large measure from new managerial approaches to the organization of service firms and institutions, coupled with new opportunities for applications of technology. To a considerable extent these advances have been made possible by the increasing size of markets and consequent increasing scale of operations. Moreover, the evidence indicates that postwar growth in services has been accomplished largely by heavy applications of labor without significant targeting on improvement in efficiency, especially in the area of coping with the heavy burden of paper work. If this is the case, there is strong likelihood that a period of vigorous rationalization lies immediately ahead.

2. There are major problems in measuring productivity in the services that are not likely to find early solution. These problems lie not only in determining units of measurement but also in taking account of changes in quality. In addition, problems in measurement grow out of demand linkages between services and goods. Where such complementarity exists and a given service stands as a critical input, its true value is extremely difficult to discern.

3. In assessing the significance of continued productivity differentials between services and goods, it is essential to distinguish private sector from public sector effects. In the private sector, maximization of efficiency is the concern of the producing firm. The buyer responds to market prices and makes such adjustment through substitution or curtailed purchase as will maximize utility (for the consumer) or cost efficiency (for the business customer). Unfavorable productivity experience in services reflected in relatively higher prices simply invites shifts to goods or to new servicing arrangements, or, when demand linkages are strong, to acceptance of high-priced services coupled with low-priced goods. By and large, neither course of action need give rise to serious consequences. In some instances, especially in producer services, the problem may be illusory: higher productivity may have been

possible only because certain highly specialized and strategic services were available.

For the public sector, adjustment is more difficult and opportunities are greater for misallocation of resources and continued voter dissatisfaction. Increased productivity must come about through new approaches to management in the public sector—approaches that begin with a definition of goals and objectives and move toward a determination of means, least cost methods, and arrangements for control and coordination.

In this light we must view the dour conclusions Baumol draws from his analysis. There has, indeed, been a critical problem of productivity in the public sector. Some progress has been made, but much remains to be done. Whether we like it or not, the public sector is deeply involved in our complex, modern civilization. It is essential that we decide what we expect of our public sector (particularly of our urban public sector), how we are to make it work effectively (that is, how to attain acceptable levels of productivity), and how we are to pay for it.

Finally, there remains the very important issue touched upon by Baumol that involves the social costs of the accommodations we make to rising relative costs caused by continuous increases in real wages in certain labor-intensive services.[16] For example, the cost of producing symphony music, ballet, and professional theater will continue to rise relative to the production of goods and services in which new techniques and technology are being applied. Accommodation will no doubt continue to emphasize increasing audience size through utilization of TV and stereo (which in a certain sense does increase productivity), substitution of amateur productions, or substitution of other less expensive forms of entertainment. Yet much is lost in these accommodations. Some of the excitement of Beethoven will be missing when one cannot be a part of the audience; the beauty and grace of the ballet cannot be duplicated in the movie house or on the TV screen; and the personal communication the talented actor establishes with his audience vanishes when mass media intervene.

But the problem is not limited to the arts. It involves a variety of services in which productivity improvement may be expected to lag: in certain (though not all) types of educational and health services, in recreational and rehabilitative services, in the care for the aged, in the maintenance of parks and buildings, and so on.

In areas where we are not content to accept the adjustments of the marketplace or the traditional assumptions regarding the appropriate scope of government, new issues arise in determining the scope of public sector responsibility. In a society where average productivity is rising, there will be opportunities for retention of the best of what was old, although we must expect that there will continue to be changes in values, in life styles, and in what we hold to be important.

4

Employment in the Services

We now examine the service work force, analyzing, first, the characteristics of service employment as measured in earnings, stability of employment, sex, and certain structural and demographic variables, and, second, the changes that are taking place with growth in service employment, in both industrial and occupational composition of the work force.

Characteristics of Service Employment (1970)

In the present section we inquire into a number of key characteristics of service employment by addressing the following questions:[1] (1) What is the distribution of service employment among well-paying, average level, and poorly paying jobs? (2) To what extent are service sector jobs part-time, part-year rather than full-time, full-year? (3) To what extent do employees in service activities find elements of job security that create satisfactory levels of earnings and stable employment? (4) How important are women workers and young and minority workers in the services and what kinds of jobs do they hold?

Distribution of Occupations between
Service and Nonservice Activities

Since we shall examine several characteristics of service employment in terms of occupational groupings, it is useful to set forth at the outset the distribution of employment between service and nonservice activities. Table 6 reveals that certain occupations (professional, semiprofessional-technical, sales workers, office and nonoffice clerical workers, and service workers) are found largely in service activities, while others (craft and kindred workers, operatives, and laborers) are found largely in nonservice activities. The classification managers-administrators is divided almost equally between the two. The table also makes clear that the occupational classification service workers pertains to a class of workers employed largely (93 percent), but not entirely, in service activities.[2]

Table 6. Distribution of Occupational Classes between Service and Nonservice Employment, 1970 (percent).

	Service	Nonservice
Professionals	79.9	20.1
Semiprofessionals	74.5	25.5
Manager-administrators	49.1	50.9
Sales workers	86.7	13.3
Craft workers	29.0	71.0
Operatives	20.5	79.4
Office clericals	70.7	29.3
Nonoffice clericals	67.3	32.7
Laborers	29.9	70.1
Service workers	92.7	7.3
Total	56.5	43.5

Source: Computed from microdata from one in a thousand sample of 1970 census of population made available by the Bureau of the Census.

The Skewed Distribution of Earnings among Service Workers

Clearly, the most striking finding regarding employment in the services is that workers are engaged to a disproportionate extent in low-income activities. This is most readily seen when service employment in each occupation is arranged into three income groups (high, medium, and low) (table 7). Distribution is heavily skewed. Well over half (56 percent) of jobs in services are found within the low-level earnings labor market segments, 27 percent in the medium level, and only 17 percent in the upper level. In sharp contrast, nonservice employment more closely approaches a normal distribution. Roughly a third (34 percent) of nonservice

Table 7. Distribution of Service Employment
among Occupation and Income Groupings, 1970.

Occupations	Distribution (%) of service employment				Principal service industries (%)*		
	All segments	High income	Medium income	Low income	High Income	Medium Income	Low Income
Professionals	15.53 (100.00)	5.46 (35.17)	10.04 (64.65)	0.03 (0.18)	Prod Serv (1.78) Health (1.19) PA (1.11)	Educ (9.97)	
Semiprofessionals	7.70 (100.00)	2.44 (31.65)	0.64 (8.34)	4.62 (60.01)	PA (2.07)		Prod Serv (0.67) Health (2.02) Educ (0.84)
Manager-administrators	9.56 (100.00)	4.67 (48.82)	4.89 (51.18)	— —	Whlsl (1.18) FIRE (1.53)	Nd Ret (2.48) PA (1.00)	
Sales workers	10.69 (100.00)	3.24 (30.27)	1.40 (13.11)	6.05 (56.62)	Whlsl (1.54) FIRE (1.69)	Dur Ret (1.40)	Nd Ret (5.50)
Craft workers	6.22 (100.00)	1.04 (16.73)	5.18 (83.27)	— —	PA (0.65)	Nd Ret (1.35) Dur Ret (1.18) Oth Cons Serv (1.56)	
Operatives	6.60 (100.00)	— —	0.52 (7.32)	6.08 (92.18)			Whlsl (1.41) Nd Ret (2.10) Oth Cons Serv (1.51)

							Industries
Office clericals	11.30 (100.00)	— —	1.46 (12.90)	9.85 (87.10)	PA	(1.46)	Whsl (0.91), Nd Ret (0.95), FIRE (2.47), Prod Serv (1.50), Health (1.09), Educ (1.95)
Nonoffice clericals	10.21 (100.00)	— —	3.02 (29.60)	7.19 (70.40)	PA	(2.41)	Nd Ret (2.39), FIRE (1.64), Educ (1.20)
Laborers	3.04 (100.00)	— —	0.29 (9.56)	2.75 (90.44)			Nd Ret (1.26)
Service workers	19.15 (100.00)	— —	— —	19.15 (100.00)			Health (4.01), Educ (2.90), Rest-Hotel (5.47), Oth Cons Serv (4.52), PA (0.63)
Total service	100.00	16.84	27.44	55.72			
Total nonservice	(100.00)	26.04	40.20	33.77			

Source: Computed from microdata from one in a thousand sample of 1970 census of population made available by the Bureau of the Census.

*Numbers in parentheses indicate percentages of total service employment accounted for.

Note: industry abbreviations: Whsl (Wholesale Trade), Nd Ret (Retail-Nondurables), Dur Ret (Retail-Durables), FIRE (Finance, Insurance, Real Estate), Prod Serv (Producer and Legal Services), Rest-Hotel (Restaurants, Hotels, Motels), Oth Cons Serv (Other Consumer Services), Health (Health Services), Educ (Education, Welfare, Nonprofit Services), PA (Public Administration).

jobs fall into the low earnings segments, 40 percent in the medium level, and 26 percent in the upper level.

When earnings are examined within occupational classes, we observe not only that certain classes tend to be, on average, better paid than others but also that there is significant variation in income among wage and salary earners within certain classes. Although professionals and managers-administrators are the highest paid groups, more than half of the individuals classified in each fall within the medium income grouping. Income of sales workers varies most widely. Thirty percent of employment is found in the high-income wholesale and FIRE subcategories where considerable knowledge of product or service sold is required, and roughly 57 percent falls in the low-income grouping dominated by the relative unskilled, nondurable, retail sales subcategory. Medium-income salesworkers fall mainly within the durable retail classification, where considerably more is typically required of the salesperson than in the retailing of nondurables. Craft employment falls predominantly in the medium-income category; and operatives, office clerical, nonoffice clerical, laborers, and service workers are largely (71 to 100 percent) in the low-income segments.

Importance of Part-time Employment in the Services

For some persons, part-time work is desirable, but for many it is not. The important observation is that where seasonal or part-time work is the characteristic condition, the worker's annual earnings are restricted.

Total earnings and the percentage of workers employed full-time, full-year (FT, FY) are closely related. When occupational classifications are examined for service employment, the low-income segments typically show smaller percentages of FT, FY than do the medium- and high-income segments (table 8).[3]

The very small percentages of full-time, full-year employment that characterize much of low-wage employment reflect factors acting upon both employers and employees. On the employers' side, work is scheduled to conform to the variations in levels of activity by drawing upon a pool of unemployed or underemployed workers as the need arises. On the employees' side, meager wages and limited fringe benefits act to reduce attachment to the job and make for frequent changes of employment interspersed with periods of idleness.

Table 8. Percentages of Workers Employed Full-Time, Full-Year within Occupational Classes, for Nonservices and Services, and Services by Income Groupings, 1970.

Occupations	All non-service	All service	High income	Medium income	Low income	Total
Professionals	78.5	47.0	73.6	32.5	63.6	
Semiprofessionals	76.3	58.4	83.1	43.0	47.5	
Manager-Administrators	79.6	81.0	79.7	82.2	—	
Sales workers	61.2	51.7	73.7	84.2	36.4	
Craft workers	62.8	71.9	80.7	70.1	—	
Operatives	54.7	51.8	—	71.4	40.1	
Office clericals	60.6	52.3	—	71.8	49.4	
Nonoffice clericals	65.7	48.0	—	66.9	40.1	
Laborers	43.7	35.3	—	67.2	31.9	
Service workers	55.4	35.7	—	—	35.7	
Total Services		51.7	77.1	57.4	41.2	
Total Nonservices	61.7		78.0	60.4	50.5	
Total employed			77.6	59.0	44.1	56.0

Source: Same as Table 6.

In general, service employment is found to be characterized by a greater proportion of part-time work than nonservice employment. Percentages of service workers employed FT, FY are smaller in all income groups, with the difference especially pronounced for the low-income segments (41.5 percent for services versus 50.5 percent for nonservice).

Extent of Sheltering in Service Employment

A variety of structural variables or attributes act under certain conditions to provide a partial sheltering effect as regards workers' wages and job security. A number of these were examined, including size of establishment, class of worker, internal labor market characteristics, existence of licensing-accreditation, and collective bargaining.

In general, a variable operates over only a part of its range or operates in varying combinations with other variables. Additional forces are at work, such as demographic variables and considerations relating to scarcity of certain types of experience or ability within the work force.

Establishment Size. Firm size has tended to increase during the postwar years and with it changes have been made in management procedures and labor-management arrangements that contribute to greater job security, including codified work rules, grievance procedures, protection against arbitrary personnel decisions, seniority arrangements for layoff and recall, and arrangements for severance pay and maintenance of employment in the face of technological change.

Increased establishment size may also act to raise the levels of responsibility and skill required of certain employees. Large organizations will tend to have higher levels of management and larger cohorts of administrators and supporting staff.[4] Nonproduction workers also tend to be more highly unionized where they are members of relatively large staffs. Yet establishment size alone may not always act to increase the annual earnings of the worker. The large establishment, especially in retailing, may make greater use of part-time workers for peak loads and relatively undemanding work.[5]

Class of worker. Worker classification (private wage and salary, government, or self-employed) need not, in and of itself, denote a degree of protection enjoyed by the jobholder, because other factors are also at work. Government employment, for example, frequently (though by no means always) provides higher annual earnings within given occupations than private sector employment. Work is likely to be more stable (that is, there is less part-time employment), and job security is enhanced through seniority rights. In recent years, government employees have tended to be more successful than their private sector counterparts in gaining wage rate increases.

Above average levels of private wage and salary employment may also be associated with more responsible jobs in large organizations, as in the case of salaried managers. Yet a high percentage of workers engaged in private wage and salary jobs (rather than self-employed) within a subgroup of the work force does not necessarily indicate either that the workers are well paid or that they are employed by large firms. To the contrary, as we shall see, very low-income workers are usually employed on a private wage and salary basis, frequently by relatively small firms.

Similarly, self-employment alone can hardly be regarded as a factor buttressing income, yet earnings among subgroups with high percentages of self-employment are frequently well above average.[6] To the extent that earnings are relatively high among these workers, the explanation would seem to lie principally in training and accreditation among professionals, experience and entrepreneurial skills among owner-managers, and skill, knowledge, and training among sales and craft workers.

Internal Labor Market. The concept of internal labor market relates to the promotional and upgrading practices within the firm. Where the internal labor market plays a major role, employees are advanced on the basis of merit and/or seniority. Outside credentialing, including educational attainment, plays a lesser role, and the degree of job security is relatively high. Such labor markets are not likely to be found in other than large firms or governments, and they need not exist for all occupations within such organizations.

Bargaining Factors. Licensing and accreditation serve to strengthen occupational distinctions and thereby to provide protection for workers where other factors such as internal labor markets are missing. There has been a strong tendency for licensing and accreditation to proliferate during the postwar period, expanding increasingly, for example, into allied health occupations.

Unions are the most important device for providing worker protection where licensing and accreditation are not possible. Greatest protection is afforded where the product or service market is well defined and least subject to rigorous competition. Unionization among white collar workers has not grown as rapidly as white collar employment, except among public employees, where it has made large gains.

Evidence of Sheltering. Table 9 summarizes the evidence relating to factors influencing sheltering. Only in certain segments of the above average (high and medium) income groupings do substantial proportions of workers in services appear to enjoy significant protection. In the high-income segments 1 and 3, these are principally professionals in producer services and health services, from licensing-accreditation (77 percent or above); in segment 2, principally managers in wholesaling and FIRE, from internal labor market (49 percent); and in segment 6, principally professionals and semiprofessionals in public administration, from very large establishment size (89 percent) and considerable internal labor market (74 percent). In the medium-income segment 7, they are principally professionals in education from licensing-accreditation (63 percent) and large establishment size (94 percent); and in segment 9, principally managers, clericals in public administration, and salesworkers in durable retailing, from very large establishment size (50 percent), considerable internal market (44 percent), and collective bargaining (36 percent).

Several above-average-earnings segments (4, 5, 8) do not appear to enjoy significant protection as a result of structural characteristics inherent in the labor market. For these, higher than average earnings may be regarded as reflecting simply the levels of responsibility or skills demanded of the workers in the jobs they hold. These segments are largely composed of managers and wholesale salespersons, whose tasks typically demand a high degree of responsibility and knowledge of products sold.

When segments with below-average earnings are examined, the picture is one of labor markets where structural characteristics provide little shelter. Workers are employed largely on a private wage and salary basis, but for the most part establishment size is small or medium; internal labor market conditions play a negligible role; and collective bargaining is of little importance. As we have seen, these below-average-earnings segments account for well over half of all service employment.

Thus the evidence indicates that service workers vary widely in the degree of sheltering against unstable employment and low wages. A minority of well-paid workers enjoy considerable protection; the large group of poorly paid workers have very little indeed.

Characteristics Relating to Sex, Age, and Race

Female Employment. In the services, women hold a much larger share of jobs (49 percent) than in nonservice activities (23

Table 9. Labor Market Segments Ranked by Mean Annual Earnings, Structural Characteristics, 1970: Service Employment Only.*

Segment rank	Self-employed	Median establishment size				Internal labor market			Bargaining factors	
		1–20	21–300	301–999	1,000+	Negligible	Moderate	Considerable	Licensing	Collective bargaining
High										
1	43.2	—	100.0	—	—	100.0	—	—	76.7	0.4
2	9.2	—	100.0	—	—	51.3	—	48.7	0.0	0.0
3	14.6	12.8	87.2	—	—	80.7	—	19.3	86.6	1.6
4	25.7	—	67.2	32.8	—	80.2	19.8	—	0.0	0.0
5	6.7	—	100.0	—	—	78.3	21.7	—	15.6	4.5
6	0.7	—	10.5	—	89.5	25.6	—	74.4	18.6	36.9
Medium										
7	2.2	5.0	1.3	93.7	—	9.2	90.8	—	62.6	26.9
8	29.9	100.0	—	—	—	100.0	—	—	1.2	1.8
9	4.1	36.6	13.7	—	49.7	44.8	10.7	44.5	1.1	36.0
10	—	—	—	—	—	—	—	—	0.0	0.0
Low										
11	3.4	9.5	90.5	—	—	75.9	5.2	18.9	2.1	1.4
12	3.3	52.3	39.0	—	8.7	100.0	—	—	0.1	32.4
13	4.4	41.8	46.9	11.1	0.1	100.0	—	—	12.6	12.4
14	5.3	42.9	30.8	26.3	—	85.6	14.4	—	8.9	12.6
Services	7.4	32.1	39.8	18.2	9.8	73.3	15.0	11.6	17.7	16.2
Nonservices	6.9	7.5	48.1	24.7	19.7	60.1	17.3	22.6	6.7	44.2

Source: Recomputed from data utilized in preparing Table 1.3, Marcia Freedman, *Labor Markets: Segments and Shelters* (Montclair, N.J.: Allanheld Osmun, 1976), p. 22. For mean earnings of segments see Table 18 below.

*Indicates percentages of those employed in service activities except in bottom row labeled "nonservices." In this row percentages relate to those employed in nonservice activities.

percent). This tendency is well established across a broad spectrum of occupations. With the single exception of the operatives classification (an important source of female employment in manufacturing), the percentages of females are higher in services than in nonservices in every occupational group (table 10).

Table 10. Women's Shares of Jobs in Service and in Nonservice Activities by Occupation, 1970 (percent).

	Service	Nonservice
Professionals	43.8	11.5
Semiprofessionals	47.5	10.5
Managers-Administrators	19.7	6.2
Sales workers	43.7	7.8
Craft workers	5.5	3.5
Operatives	24.2	33.4
Office clericals	91.5	86.1
Nonoffice clericals	62.5	45.0
Laborers	11.5	7.2
Service workers	66.7	18.5
Total Services	48.8	
Total Nonservices		22.8

Source: Same as Table 6.

Important though this observation may be, it fails to focus on an even more significant characteristic of female employment: the tendency to restrict the types of employment open to women and to employ them to a disproportionate extent in low-wage jobs (table 11). The concentration of female employment in the low-income segments is exceedingly high, 74 percent. Employment as clerical and service workers accounts for the major part of these low-income jobs although substantial numbers also hold jobs as salesworkers (nondurable retailing) and semiprofessionals-technicians (health and education).

This distribution stands in sharp contrast to the distribution of males (table 11). The percentage of male workers in the low-income services segments is less, 38 percent, and the percentages in the middle- and upper-income segments (especially the upper) are much higher, 34 and 28 percent, respectively (versus 20 and 6 percent for women).

Table 11. Distribution of Male and Female Service Employment among Occupation and Income Groupings, 1970 (percent).

	Female				Male			
	Total	High income	Medium income	Low income	Total	High income	Medium income	Low income
Professionals	13.9	2.1	11.8	0.0	17.1	8.7	8.3	0.0
Semiprofessionals	7.5	0.4	0.5	6.6	7.9	4.4	0.8	2.8
Managers-administrators	3.9	2.0	1.9	—	15.0	7.2	7.8	—
Sales workers	9.6	0.9	0.4	8.3	11.8	5.5	2.4	3.9
Craftworkers	0.7	0.1	0.6	—	11.5	2.0	9.5	—
Operatives	3.3	—	0.3	2.9	9.8	—	0.7	9.1
Office clericals	21.2	—	2.6	18.6	1.9	—	0.4	1.5
Nonoffice clericals	13.1	—	2.2	10.9	7.5	—	3.8	3.7
Laborers	0.7	—	0.0	0.7	5.3	—	0.5	4.7
Service workers	26.2	—	—	26.2	12.5	—	—	12.5
Total	100.0	5.5	20.4	74.1	100.0	27.7	34.1	38.2

Source: Same as Table 6.

Young workers. An initial observation is that workers under twenty-five years of age are overrepresented in service employment (22 percent of service employment is accounted for by workers under twenty-five years of age compared to only 16 percent of nonservice employment). This means that by 1970 the services offered the greatest job opportunities for the young in contrast to an earlier era, when a majority of those entering the work force—at that time largely males—found early employment in farm and factory work.

Not unexpectedly, in both services and nonservices most workers under twenty-five are in low-income employment. A larger percentage of service workers than of nonservice workers are found in this grouping, however.

Income Grouping	Service	Nonservice
High	6.1%	14.1%
Medium	19.4	18.5
Low	74.5	67.4
	100.0%	100.0%

Of special interest is the fact that almost two-thirds (63 percent) of young service workers are employed within labor market segments where collective bargaining coverage is less than 13 percent and only 19 percent within segments in which the level of collective bargaining is as much as 32 percent.[7] In contrast, among young nonservice workers, roughly 60 percent of unemployment falls within segments where collective bargaining coverage is quite high (above 50 percent).[8]

The data for workers under twenty-five years of age have not been broken down by sex, but, because employment of young service workers, both male and female, is so heavily weighted toward the low-income segments, we can readily visualize the major types of work performed by each. Young women are most likely to find jobs as clerical and service workers and as sales workers in nondurable retailing. Young men will tend to be employed as service workers, operatives, laborers, and, to a lesser extent, as nonoffice clericals and nondurable retail sales workers.

Nonwhites. Nonwhites are somewhat more heavily represented in both the lower-income and the higher-income segments in service than in nonservice activities and somewhat less heavily represented in the medium-income segments.

Segments	Service	Nonservice
High	6.1%	4.8%
Medium	10.0	13.0
Low	16.0	15.1

But service employment is, itself, disproportionately low income, and, accordingly, a much larger percentage of nonwhites who work in services are in the low-income segments (71 percent) than are the nonwhites who work in the nonservice activities (48 percent).

A Profile of the Service Work Force

At this point, a profile begins to emerge of the services work force in which the dominant characteristics are: (1) a disproportionately large number of workers (56 percent) in below-average-earnings segments, with over two-fifths in segments with annual earnings averaging less than 60 percent of the labor force mean; (2) strong tendencies toward part-time employment, with scarcely more than two-fifths of those workers in below-average-earnings segments working FT, FY; (3) protective structural factors that are of considerable importance for groups of well-paid professionals and managers in the highest income segments and for certain public sector employees, but only weakly operative, or negligible, for most remaining workers; (4) a disproportionately large number of female jobs that tend to be concentrated in a restricted group of predominantly ill-paid occupational categories; (5) an overrepresentation of young and minority workers who tend to find less-well-paying employment and less job security than in nonservice activities.

Employment Growth and Change

These insights into the composition and special characteristics of service employment at the beginning of the 1970s, though

57

valuable, tell us little about the remarkable transformation that has been at work within the employed labor force.

The two following sections examine this transformation, considering, first, changes in employment that occurred during the decade of the sixties, and, second, changes that have occurred during the present decade up to 1977. The treatment of the sixties is much more complete because it makes use of census of population materials that break down employment by occupations *within* industrial groupings, while that of the seventies is based on separate occupational and industrial employment data.[9]

The 1960–1970 Employment Transformation

The following discussion is based on an analysis in which both male and female employment changes are subdivided into four categories (table 12): (1) changes that would have occurred if employment had grown at the national rate within each industry, with sex and occupational ratios held constant; (2) additional gains (or losses) in employment that would have been expected in sex-occupational subgroups as a result of individual industry growth rates (here 1960 sex and occupational composition within industries were again held constant); and (3) changes in employment in specific sex-occupational subgroups due to "shift" (that is, changes caused by increased or decreased percentage of employment accounted for by occupation or sex within individual industries); (4) net change, by occupation.

A word of explanation regarding interpretation of the results is in order. In industries that grew at rates above the national rates, the changes in the second category ("expected" additional gains—or losses—due to industry growth) are positive, but in industries that grew at less than the national rate, the changes in the second category are negative. The third category is made up of "shift," changes not explained by industry growth. Changes may be positive (growth in employment in the sex-occupational subgroup exceeded "expected") or negative (growth was less than "expected"). A positive change in the third category with a negative change in the second simply means that employment in the sex-occupational subgroups exceeded the change expected on the

Table 12. Analysis of Employment Change by Occupation, Industry, and Sex, 1960 to 1970.

Occupation	Gain at National Growth Rate	"Expected" Additional Gain (Loss) due to Industry Growth†	Industry Nonservices* "Shift," Additional Gain (Loss)‡	Net Change	1970 Employment share %
Male	6,160.3	-4,166.7	-1,032.8	960.8	77.6
Professional, technical	420.1	-193.1	509.2	736.2	7.3
Managers, administrators	393.4	-151.3	-33.9	208.2	5.4
Sales workers	163.4	-65.2	-179.6	-81.4	1.7
Clerical workers	342.1	-132.1	-92.5	117.5	4.5
Craft workers	1,607.8	-565.1	13.6	1,056.3	22.7
Operatives	1,710.5	-812.0	-574.5	324.0	21.7
Laborers	538.3	-221.2	-471.2	-154.1	6.1
Farm workers	895.6	-1,989.4	-352.7	-1,446.5	6.5
Service workers	89.1	-37.3	148.8	200.6	1.7
Female	1,418.7	-723.9	1,032.8	1,727.6	22.4
Professional, technical	38.4	-16.1	118.2	140.5	0.9
Managers, administrators	22.5	-9.2	17.3	30.6	0.4
Sales workers	17.6	-7.8	-3.2	6.6	0.2
Clerical workers	510.0	-196.9	296.5	609.6	8.0
Craft workers	40.2	-15.3	135.4	160.3	1.0
Operatives	661.1	-260.9	395.0	795.2	10.4
Laborers	17.1	-7.6	61.4	70.9	0.4
Farm workers	90.1	-200.1	-26.9	-136.9	0.7
Service workers	21.7	-10.0	39.1	50.8	0.4
Total	7,579.0	-4,890.6	0.0	2,688.4	100.0
Nonservices					43.2

Table 12. (continued)

Occupation	Gain at National Growth Rate	*Industry Services**[*]		
		"Expected" Additional Gain (Loss) due to Industry Growth[†]	*"Shift," Additional Gain (Loss)*[‡]	*Net Change*	*1970 Employment share %*
Male				
Professional, technical	4,155.5	2,593.1	−1,433.3	5,315.3	50.5
Managers, administrators	695.1	1,111.7	−212.1	1,594.7	10.1
Sales workers	757.0	291.5	−551.9	496.6	8.1
Clerical workers	576.9	254.8	−415.0	416.7	6.3
Craft workers	408.1	219.7	−110.0	517.8	5.0
Operatives	505.3	299.0	−241.2	563.1	6.0
Laborers	440.2	135.8	−210.6	365.4	4.9
Farm workers	200.5	49.3	90.0	339.8	2.6
Service workers	572.4	231.3	217.5	1,021.2	7.6

Table 12. (continued)

Female					
Professional, technical	646.4	1,299.9	–281.8	1,664.5	9.8
	3,550.6	2,298.7	1,433.3	7,282.6	49.5
Managers, administrators	170.9	65.8	12.7	249.4	2.1
Sales workers	395.8	84.6	–2.7	477.7	4.7
Clerical workers	1,054.9	889.9	1,279.4	3,224.2	17.1
Craft workers	22.6	9.3	77.4	109.3	0.5
Operatives	149.7	–34.0	–13.9	101.8	1.6
Laborers	8.7	3.0	97.7	109.4	0.3
Farm workers	—	—	—	—	—
Service workers	1,101.6	–19.8	264.5	1,346.3	13.2
Total	7,706.1	4,891.8	0.0	12,597.9	100.0
Services					56.8

* Numbers of gain (loss) are in thousands.

† Gains (losses) due to growth at industry rates with fixed occupation-sex composition. These data are prepared separately for each industry and results netted. Where the individual industry grows at more (less) than the national average, there will be a gain (loss) (i.e., "expected" growth will be more [less] than estimated growth at national rate).

‡ Change greater (less) than "expected." See text for further explanation.

Source: U.S. Bureau of the Census, Census of Population, *Detailed Characteristics,* PC (1), Volume I (Washington, D.C.: U.S. Government Printing Office, 1972).

basis of industry growth rates, but industry growth rates were less than the national rate.

Two general observations can be made. First, service employment grew much more rapidly than that in nonservices. For services, there was an increase of employment of 4.9 million in excess of gains that would have been made if these activities had grown at the overall (average) national rate; for nonservices, there was a corresponding deficiency of 4.9 million jobs. Second, female employment growth in the services was greater than in nonservice activities. In part this was because female employment in the services was relatively large even in 1960. If both service and nonservice employment had grown at the national average and the percentage of women had been held constant, there would have been an increase of 3.6 million female jobs in services compared to 1.4 million in nonservice activities. But total service employment grew much more rapidly than nonservice employment, and a large share of additional jobs for women resulted simply from higher rates of service employment growth. Controlling for sex and occupational composition, differentials in service sector growth would have accounted for 2.3 million more female jobs than would have opened up at national growth rates. The relatively slow growth of nonservice activities, on the other hand, would have resulted in a shortfall of 724,000 female jobs measured against gains that would have been made if individual industries had grown at the overall national rate.

But over and beyond this gain, there was a shift from male to female employment within the service sector (caused by increased shares of female employment within individual industry groups) that accounted for an additional 1.4 million jobs and a somewhat smaller shift toward female employment in nonservice activities amounting to slightly over 1 million jobs.

The analysis of male and female employment gains by occupation provides additional information, especially as regards employment growth in the three occupational groupings that accounted for the major shares of the total increase of 12.6 million service jobs during the sixties: professional, semiprofessional-technical workers (officially designated as professional, technical, and kindred or PTK), clerical workers, and service workers.

Professional-Technical-Kindred. This occupational group is of special interest in view of the heavy emphasis that has been given to the rising importance of professional and technical workers in the new "service" or "postindustrial" society. During the sixties, the rapid growth in PTK employment in services was principally associated with the rapid growth of certain service industry categories in which this occupational grouping holds a large share of employment. But PTK employment, though of major importance, did not grow as rapidly as all employment in the service industrial classifications. There was a negative shift of 212,000 males and 282,000 females.

This negative shift was, however, confined entirely to one broad industrial category, principally health and educational services, but including also welfare, nonprofit, and religious organizations. In the remaining service industrial categories, shifts were positive and substantially offsetting, as will be seen in table 13, which analyzes, by industry, PTK employment changes over and beyond those that would have been accounted for at national growth rates.

Table 13. Employment Changes in Service Industries: Professional, Technical, and Kindred Occupations, 1960 to 1970.

	"Expected" additional gains (losses) due to industry growth (in thousands)*		Additional gains (losses) due to "shift" (in thousands)*	
	Male	*Female*	*Male*	*Female*
Health, education, etc.	1,063.1	1,295.2	−475.3	−438.1
Wholesale	10.7	1.4	34.6	9.7
FIRE	13.7	3.4	33.5	28.9
Business, repair service	28.6	6.8	66.8	39.9
Retail	5.6	1.5	27.3	31.0
Entertainment-recreation	−39.2	−16.3	21.2	28.9
Public administration	29.2	7.9	79.8	17.9
Total	1,111.7	1,299.9	−212.1	−281.8

* See table 12 for further explanation and source.

There was also significant growth in total PTK employment in the nonservice industrial categories (not shown on table 13 and principally manufacturing), total net changes amounting to 877,000 jobs (27 percent of comparable service sector gains). Here relatively rapid gains were *not* associated with industry employment expansion, because employment for the nonservices as a whole grew at less than the national rate. Thus in both nonservices and services (with the important exception of the health-education category) professional and technical occupations grew in *relative* importance during the sixties.

Clerical workers. For the economy as a whole, gains in clerical employment were even greater than in the PTK grouping. The increased employment of women as clerical workers was the single most important factor in the transformation within the service work force. During the sixties, in service industries, clerical employment among females increased by 3.2 million jobs, 1.3 million of which were accounted for by shift. Among males, however, there was a decline in relative importance of clerical employment in service industries with a negative shift of 110,000, although there was a net gain of over a half million male clerical jobs.

Just what was taking place at the industry level is made clear in table 14, showing service employment changes in numbers of clerical workers in excess of gains that would have been made at the national growth rate.

Table 14. Employment Changes in Service Industries: Clerical Workers, 1960 to 1970.

	"Expected" additional gains (losses) due to industry growth (in thousands)*		Additional gains (losses) due to "shift" (in thousands)*	
	Male	*Female*	*Male*	*Female*
Health, education, etc.	63.6	547.6	43.7	450.5
Wholesale	33.4	58.6	−33.4	41.8
FIRE	53.2	186.8	−52.1	95.1
Business, repair service	16.5	57.0	10.6	78.9
Retail	12.3	36.8	39.0	481.7
Entertainment-recreation	−15.3	−54.6	20.5	118.5
Public administration	56.0	57.7	−138.3	12.9
Total	219.7	889.9	−110.0	1,279.4

* See Table 12 for further explanation and source.

The shift toward increased importance of female clerical employment characterized every service industrial grouping. In health-education, the positive shift of almost a half-million clerical jobs occurred in the face of the large negative shift in PTK service industry jobs observed above. Of equal interest is the very substantial shift (39,000 males, 482,000 females) toward increased clerical employment in retailing occurring alongside negative shifts (not shown on the table) in managers (485,000 males, 55,000 females), salesworkers (310,000 males, 89,000 females), and operatives (100,000 males). Again, in the declining entertainment-recreation grouping, there were significant shifts favoring clerical jobs (20,000 males, 118,000 females) in the face of sizable negative shifts in female service workers (see below) and in male and female operatives (not shown).

In nonservices, as in services, we observe (table 12) the same tendency for negative shifts to reduce the significance of clerical employment among men and for strong positive shifts to increase clerical job opportunities for women.

Service Workers. The occupational category service workers was the third most important source of employment gains in the services. Employment increased in these activities by 2.4 million, with the major share, 1.7 million, accounted for by growth at the national rate and additional increases totaling 212,000 accounted for by above average industry growth rates. The net increase due to shift was 482,000 (218,000 males, 264,000 females). Not shown in table 12 were important interoccupational shifts within service industries, especially among females. In entertainment-recreation, there was a negative shift of 193,000 female service workers at the same time that a positive shift of 118,000 female clerical jobs was occurring (see above). In the health-education grouping, however, there was a substantial positive shift (335,000) toward increased employment of women as service workers as well as the shift toward increased numbers of clerical workers (see above), while the relative importance of PTK employment declined through negative shift for both males and females. Among males there were shifts toward greater employment of service workers in every service industrial category except FIRE and health-education.

In nonservices, the service worker category showed positive shifts for both males and females in all major categories.

Recent trends (1970–1977)

It is clear from the preceding analysis that an understanding of occupational changes must involve a factoring out of the effects of industry growth and that the use of occupational or industry data alone may result in misinterpretation of trends in employment composition. It is also clear that the broad occupational groupings that must be used for most trend studies are extremely heterogeneous in terms of income and levels of skill. This lack of appropriate classification has led to certain misconceptions regarding skill-income composition of service employment. The most common, and certainly the most mischievous, is that the PTK grouping is composed entirely of fairly highly skilled and well-paid professionals. But, as we have observed, when the occupational class is properly subdivided and employment is specified by industry and sex, this is by no means the case.

In spite of an absence of cross-classification of the industry and occupational data and appropriate controls for distinguishing between national, industrial, and occupational growth trends, analysis of *Current Population Survey* employment estimates classified separately by industry and occupation does provide a number of insights regarding changes under way within the economy since 1970. The following would appear to be the most important:

1. Trends toward more rapid growth in service than nonservice employment, more rapid growth in female than male jobs, and a disproportionate share of female jobs opening up in services have continued. Eighty-six percent of all job increases from 1970 to 1977 were in the service industry classes, and 54 percent of all job increases were accounted for by female employment.[10] Among female job increases, 91 percent were in service jobs; of male job increases, 79 percent.

2. The growth in service employment has been broadly based in terms of industrial groupings. With the exception of federal government, personal services, and private household services, employment in all service industrial categories has grown at above the national rate. The largest contributions in shares of total job increases were retailing, 23.2 percent, medical and hospital

services, 12.8 percent, and educational services, 12.4 percent. Highest annual rates of employment growth were found in the more detailed industry classes, eating and drinking places, 6.0 percent, welfare-religious services, 7.8 percent, and other professional services, 7.1 percent.

3. There is evidence of continued changes in the occupational composition of employment in major service industrial groupings. Employment of retail sales workers declined in spite of an overall growth of almost 3 percent per annum in retailing. It is likely that the offsetting increases are to be found largely among managers-administrators, stenographers-typists, and service workers, reflecting new modes of operation as self-service and use of electronic checkout technology increase in importance.[11]

Similarly, employment of health workers and teachers grew less rapidly than total employment in health and education. Here again, it is likely that the offsetting gains are to be found largely by increased employment of office clericals made necessary by new administrative requirements and by procedures related to third-party payments.

4. There appears to have been some upgrading of employment for women. The most striking change occurred in the salaried managers-administrators category, where growth occurred at a rate of over 10 percent per annum and accounted for 12 percent of all female employment gains. Here we are observing the new trend toward hiring young women in a variety of junior managerial positions, the most visible cases being in the banks and headquarters offices of large corporations. A second source of upgrading appears to have been PTK occupational employment, which accounted for almost 18 percent of female job increases. Female employment in this occupational group grew at the rate of 3.6 percent, over twice the national rate for all employment and well above the overall rate for women. Although it is likely that most of these new jobs were not in top-level professional positions, in general, they represent better than average career opportunities for women.

On the other hand, 31 percent of female job increases were accounted for by clerical workers, 28 percent by service workers, and the remaining 11 percent by craft workers, sales workers, and laborers. For the most part, these occupations pay no better than average wages.

5. For males there were significant occupational shifts, but it is not clear that there was an overall upgrading of jobs. The PTK grouping, representing better than average jobs as a whole, accounted for over 14 percent of job increases. Here the share of men's jobs rose from 12.9 in 1970 to 13.5 in 1977. On the other hand, the service worker occupational classification, representing for the most part poorer jobs, accounted for over 28 percent of job creation, rising from 7.4 to 9.9 percent of the total male employment. It is interesting to observe that within the latter occupational group considerable transformation is taking place. Almost a fifth of male job increases in services (almost 6 percent of total male job increases) were accounted for by growth of employment in the very small industrial subclass, protective services, because private sector security forces were enlarged throughout the economy. In addition, the managers-administrators occupational group is of special interest in that there was a shift from self-employed to salaried status, related, presumably, to increased importance of large-scale multiunit retail and fast food enterprises. There is no evidence, however, that this represented an upgrading of employment.

Other shifts in male employment of less importance include a decline in the share of clerical workers and a rise in importance of sales workers outside of retailing. Small gains in numbers of craft workers and laborers largely involved changes in occupational structure within nonservice activities.

Employment Gains in Service-Type Occupations: Services and Nonservices Compared

In Chapter 1 it was pointed out that in studying services we are concerned only with those private and public sector organizations that have services as their output. Yet servicelike functions are performed within nonservice as well as service organizations.

The analysis of employment change in table 12 permits us to make rough estimates of the extent to which such shifts toward servicelike functions are accounted for by the service sector, at least to the extent that these changes are revealed by changes in broad occupational categories during the sixties. The classifications professional-technical, managers-administrators, sales workers, clerical workers, and service workers may be considered to be typically associated with the performance of servicelike functions regardless of the hiring organization. When 1960–70 changes in employment (male and female combined) in these occupations are summed separately for services and nonservices the results are as follows:

	Nonservices (000's)	Services (000's)
Professional, technical	+876.7	+3,259.2
Managers-administrators	+238.8	+746.0
Sales workers	−74.8	+894.0
Clerical workers	+727.1	+3,742.0
Service workers	+251.4	+2,367.5
Total	+2,019.2 (15.5%)	+13,028.3 (84.5%)

Clearly the lion's share of growth in those jobs associated with white collar and other servicelike work is taking place within the service sector. We must note, however, that nonservice activities have also been involved in a lively transition. Employment in service-type occupations increased by over two millions in nonservices during the sixties although total employment increased by only 2.7 million.

The general conclusion to be drawn is that the transformation toward more and more employment in servicelike functions is occurring everywhere, but that it is taking place predominantly through growth in the service sector.

Summary and Conclusions

This analysis has dealt, first, with the structure of the service work force, considering earnings distribution, sex and demographic composition, and structural factors acting to influence job security, and, second, with the transformation taking place within the economy that is leading not simply to larger service employment but to increased importance of women and to changes in the relative importance of various occupations.

Contrary to much that has been said, the service work force is not, on average, better paid or more highly skilled than the nonservice work force. Rather, it is characterized by a larger proportion of workers at the lower end of the earnings scale, by a higher proportion of women and minority workers, by higher percentages of part-time employment, and by fewer structural and institutional arrangements that enhance job security. Nevertheless, among professionals and managers, salaries in the upper range of the distribution of incomes are quite high, and job security is maximized through licensing, accreditation, and the possession of highly developed and much needed skills. It is here and in the top managerial positions of large industrial firms that we find the elite of the labor force.

Growth in services and growth in female employment have been closely associated. Of the total increase of 9.0 million female jobs between 1960 and 1970, 7.3 million were in services. Only 5.9 million of these increases in female jobs could be accounted for simply by growth rates that obtained in the respective service activities. The remaining increase of 1.4 million new jobs represents an enlargement of the role of women in the services brought about through changes in composition of service employment that have favored women.

Transformations have occurred in every major industrial classification within the services. Fundamentally, they represent new manpower requirements growing out of new ways of getting work done and new types of services being offered. In retailing, for example, sales workers have become less important while other occupations, principally clerical workers and service workers, have become relatively more important. In the health-education industrial classification, the professional-technical occupations failed to grow at as rapid a rate as total employment during the sixties (although they accounted for the major share of growth), while other occupational groupings, principally clerical and service workers, grew more rapidly.

For most of the service industries, the three occupational groups, clerical, professional-technical, and service workers, have increased in relative importance. In general, these changes have favored women over men: almost all gains in clerical jobs have gone to women, as have somewhat more than half of all increases in professional-technical and service worker jobs.[12]

Taken as a whole, the evidence does not point to a generalized trend toward more highly skilled occupations or higher levels of individual income. To the extent that women have increased their role in the professional-technical occupations (and as managers and administrators in the seventies), they may be presumed to have improved their relative earnings, although the positions gained have been largely as semiprofessionals and technicians, with some recent significant gains as professionals, particularly as doctors and lawyers. Even increases in clerical jobs at the expense of sales jobs (largely in nondurable retailing) have probably served to raise wage levels. But it must be remembered that women have traditionally earned less than men and that such improvement serves mainly to reduce unfavorable earnings differentials.

The position of men is more ambiguous. Although there was a decline during the sixties in the relative importance of professional-technical jobs in health-education as measured by the shift analysis, this occupational category has continued to be a major source of job expansion. Professional-technical employment of men increased by almost 1.6 million jobs during the sixties and has continued to increase at a higher than national rate during the seventies. In general, men have a preferred earnings status within this group of occupations. On the other hand, the fact that the second most important source of employment expansion among males has been within the service worker occupational group indicates clearly that a large number of jobs on the low end continue to open up.

These findings raise the difficult question about what it means to live in a society where jobs are predominantly in the service sector, women play a more important role, a large share of work is part time, and the earnings structure tends to be skewed unfavorably.

One can make a strong case that such a set of conditions will lead to a new set of career expectations and standards for successful achievement. With both men and women in the labor market, emphasis will shift from the earnings of a single breadwinner to the combined earnings of two and from maximizing earnings opportunities for one to creating the best arrangement for both parties to find rewarding work. Moreover, when all this occurs under conditions of postponed childbearing and very small families, the central city takes on a new appeal. It is unlikely that a whole generation of middle-class young people reared in the suburbs will find it congenial to relocate in the city, but there are powerful attractions for many in living where the range of jobs is largest, where home and work place are in close proximity, and where cultural, educational, and recreational opportunities are the most varied.

These speculations bring us, finally, to a set of questions involving the location of service jobs. What is the role of cities relative to suburbs and nonmetropolitan places in terms of service employment expansion? What types of cities are favored? To what extent may the industrial-occupational composition of service jobs be expected to vary from place to place? These are the questions to be addressed in Chapter 5.

5

The Urbanization of Services

An initial premise in discussing the location of services is that goods and services are distinguished largely by the fact that the former can typically be stored and shipped whereas the latter cannot. Thus, service firms tend to locate as close to customers as is feasible, whereas goods-producing firms may respond to any of a number of factors such as labor costs, proximity to raw materials or suppliers, and accessibility to regional or national markets. This is an important insight, but it alone cannot explain the spatial distribution of services or the role services play in determining the size and industrial composition of metropolitan and nonmetropolitan places. An explanation of why some services are virtually ubiquitous while others are found in relatively few places is needed.

Central Place Theory and the Hierarchy of Services

The branch of economic theory that deals with the spatial distribution of service firms in a free enterprise economy is called "central place theory." It seeks to explain the size and spatial organization of firms according to certain factors that determine the size of market each firm can carve out for itself. Stated briefly, market size is determined by three factors working together:

economies of scale in the production processes, *extent of demand*, and *transportation costs* (the delivery costs to seller or buyer). Scale economies dictate the size a firm must attain to compete: a department store with its wide variety of merchandise must have a larger marketing area than a delicatessen or barber shop because the minimum efficient size of its physical facilities, inventories, and staff will be larger. Further, where populations are sparse or family incomes are low, market areas must be more far-flung than where populations are dense and incomes are high. Finally, where transport costs between buyer and seller are high (for example, where terrain is difficult or efficient modes of transport are not available), the firms will tend to be located closer to customers than where costs are low; witness the need for the small local grocery store in the days before the automobile.[1] The factor of transport costs is secondary, however, to the need for a marketing area to be large enough to sustain the service organization.

According to central place theory, services may best be viewed in terms of minimum necessary size ("threshold" size) of markets. Activities with small market thresholds (called low-level activities), such as grocery stores, gasoline service stations, and eating places, will be the only ones to group together in hamlets, villages, or even residential clusters within cities or suburbs (that is, in low-level places); and there will be many such places. Activities with larger market thresholds (higher level activities), such as furniture stores, hotels, or photo studios, tend to be grouped in places no smaller than towns or small cities. These larger (and higher level) central places will be fewer in number yet will include activities found in the smallest market areas. As we move to increasingly larger cities, more complex and highly specialized activities are added, because they operate successfully only in the midst of more extensive markets. These larger places are even fewer in number and replicate the entire range of activities found in the smaller sized places.

Thus, in central place theory, the national economy is visualized as composed of a hierarchy of metropolitan places a small number of which are very large, a large number middle sized, and a larger number small, all engaged in producing services that can be viewed hierarchically—the hierarchy of services providing the functional basis for the hierarchy of urban places. The corollary statement is that each urban place can be visualized as exporting certain services to its hinterland, including places lower in the hierarchy, and importing services produced by places even higher in the hierarchy in addition to goods and specialized services, such as government, from elsewhere in the outside economy. At the same time, both large and small urban economies include within their industrial complex a number of low-level "local sector" services, such as grocery stores, service stations, and drug stores, that provide for the needs of residents.

Modification of the Theory: Other Considerations

In its simplest form, this theory is applicable primarily to the spatial organization of consumer service firms where the population is fairly widely and evenly dispersed. Its validity has been tested in rural areas of the Middle West, where cities, towns, and hamlets are arranged in a well-established hierarchy.[2]

In practice, firms often differentiate their products or services from those of competing firms and locate near such competitors. One firm may feature low prices for cash merchandise, another will extend credit and offer better quality, still another will feature a wider variety of goods. Indeed, firms with closely competing goods or services located near one another provide the customer with an opportunity to make quality and price comparisons. Such deliberate differentiation of products, along with the spatial overlapping of markets, tends to occur in urbanized areas with concentrated populations. Here a firm need not reach out for its clientele, because its relatively dense market is smaller in area and transport costs are low.

Moreover, large places will have a greater variety of services even within the local sector. One reason is that the increased size of the local market permits a higher degree of specialization, so that the consumer is offered a wider range of choice among recreation facilities, types of stores, and cultural attractions. On the other hand, large city life styles and living requirements are likely to be somewhat different. There will be a greater need for parking garages, public transportation, and specialized public sector services (for example, special types of building inspectors and fire fighting for high-rise buildings).

In contrast, where populations are scattered or transport costs are high, the sales potential may be too small to permit the sharing of markets and the differentiation of products and services. In such areas, the range of services will be smaller and the system will be "rationalized" by economic necessity so that each firm has a virtual monopoly in its own market area. This condition describes, of course, the marketing structure of much of nineteenth-century rural America and of many underdeveloped regions today.

Thus, market structure tends to be different in urbanized and in rural areas, although it is essentially hierarchical in both. Central place theory, emphasizing minimum size of market necessary for efficient operation, is applicable in both urban and rural areas.

The theory fails to deal explicitly with producer services and with services in the not-for-profit sector but is readily expanded to correct this deficiency. Business and not-for-profit services are also hierarchical with regard to market size required for efficient operaton. High-level services tend to be highly specialized and frequently require skilled professionals as well as considerable investment in equipment and sometimes in plant to render the service in question (for example, the highly sophisticated legal firm, investment house, medical center, or university). Accordingly, extensive markets are needed to justify them economically, and their services are to a large extent exported. There will be relatively few urban centers in which the very highest level of services are located, and they will typically be large. Conversely, lower level business and not-for-profit services will be less specialized and will require smaller markets. It follows that there will be more urban centers in which these lower level activities are located. As in the case of consumer services, these lower level producers and not-for-profit sector services will be found in both the smallest and the largest places: local sector activities of all kinds are replicated at all higher levels of the urban size-of-place hierarchy.

Agglomeration Linkages among Service Activities and the System of Metropolitan Economies

But the relatively restricted concepts embodied in central place theory do not describe adequately the forces that have worked together to build the modern metropolis. The growth of services in urban economies occurs not simply through firms making independent responses to demand forces in terms of necessary market size. Rather, a dynamic process of agglomeration works to attract activities to one another, bringing about a spatial organization in which a group of service activities tend to be concentrated and organized in such a way as to emphasize proximity.

This is most readily illustrated by the location characteristics of business services and corporate headquarters operations in certain of our larger cities. In Chapter 2 we saw that service firms existing as independent units are frequently able to perform functions with greater expertise and at lower cost than their customers could perform such functions "in-house." What was not emphasized was the process by which opportunities to take advantage of such "external economies" attract user firms, especially headquarters operations of large firms, to locate close at hand; and that the presence of those firms, in turn, increases the size of market and encourages the development of still other specialized firms, increasing yet again the locational attractiveness of the city.

Moreover, just as business firms spring up in response to increasing size of the market, so do a host of private and public sector services: hotels, restaurants, theaters, transportation terminals, medical centers, art galleries, and a large variety of specialized shops. These, in turn, encourage further agglomeration by making the city a more attractive place to locate.

Thus a description of agglomerative processes reinforces the logic of central place theory by providing a description of processes that bring together activities at each level of the urban hierarchy.

There are many activities whose location in cities cannot be satisfactorily described by the above sketches of some of the interdependencies at work in the larger central place type of metropolitan economy. Manufacturing, resort, even certain government, transshipment, or educational activities may be located chiefly in response to the need to be close to sources of input or to major transportation terminals, in response to climatic or other environmental advantages, or because historical accident has dictated that a certain place shall host a government or university center. Such cities are not central places in the sense that they provide a variety of services to a hinterland. Rather, they are "specialized" places whose principal function is to produce and sell a narrow range of goods or services to the outside world, typically to distant markets or to customers who may come from distant places. Even these specialized places provide, however, an array of lower order, central place type of services to their own residents and, to some extent, to the immediately surrounding area.

Thus, the entire system of towns, cities, and metropolitan areas must be seen as comprised, on one hand, of general service centers (which we shall call "nodal" places) and, on the other, of specialized places. What they have in common is that each is a complex urban economy that exports goods or services to outside markets and, in turn, imports from other areas. Moreover, each provides its own residents with a variety of lower order, local sector, central place type of services.

Empirical Evidence Regarding the System of Metropolitan Economies

Variations among Metropolitan Areas in Industrial Composition of Employment

All this means that metropolitan economies may be expected to be alike in some respects and significantly different in others. In terms of local sector activities, most places should have similar shares of employment in basic services (for example, grocery stores and service stations), although some places such as resort centers may have more. In terms of specialized, export-oriented activities such as advertising, finance, accounting, and manufacturing, employment shares in some places would be expected to be relatively large and in others, relatively small.

Table 15 provides evidence of such characteristics by showing the extent to which shares of employment in specific industries varied among the 259 standard metropolitan statistical areas (SMSAs) within the American economy in 1970. The measure used, the coefficient of variation, expresses the extent of variation among shares of employment in a given industrial class relative to the average share of employment (all SMSAs) in that class.[3] Where shares of total employment accounted for by a given industry show little variation among places, it can be assumed that the activity is more or less ubiquitous. On the other hand, where variation is relatively great, it can be presumed that places with relatively large shares are exporting and those with relatively small shares are importing the output of the industry in question.

The coefficient for "other transportation," for example (largely airports and marine port activity) is 0.72, whereas for food and drug stores it is 0.15. Thus, port activities have relatively large shares of employment in some SMSAs, where they represent an important element of the export complex, but not in others. Food and drug stores, on the other hand, are required everywhere to provide for the needs of residents and thus are largely, though by no means entirely, local sector activities. (In some places, such as resort and service centers, they are, at least in part, export activities.)

The analysis sheds considerable light on the location characteristics of business services. FIRE, wholesaling, and communications have relatively low coefficients that are, nevertheless, significantly higher than retail trade. In part, they are local sector activities, for they provide for the needs of consumers and local tradesmen. In part, however, they belong to the export sector, for they serve the needs of firms within the export sector of the metropolis and of other firms and institutions located elsewhere within the national and international economies.

Classification of SMSAs

In a recent study, I collaborated in classifying each SMSA according to a typology based on export specialization as suggested by industrial composition of employment.[4] Approximately

Table 15. Variation in Shares of Employment among 259 SMSAs, 1970:
Coefficients of Variation, Selected Industrial Groupings.*

Industry	Coefficients of Variation	
Primary	0.91	
Agriculture and agricultural services		0.93
Forestry and fisheries		1.85
Mining		2.65
Construction	0.25	
Manufacturing	0.47	
Transportation	0.45	
Railroads and railway express		1.17
Trucking and warehousing		0.41
Other transportation		0.72
Communications	0.33	
Utilities	0.40	
Services		
Wholesale trade		0.36
Finance, insurance, and real estate		0.33
Business and repair services		0.39
Retail trade		0.12
Food and dairy products stores		0.15
Eating and drinking places		0.22
Other retail trade		0.13
Recreation		0.52
Lodging places		0.47
Entertainment		1.01
Private household		0.52
Medical and education		0.29
Government	1.04	
Administration		0.58
Armed forces		2.24

Source: Data were compiled from computer tapes containing data published in L. D. Ashby and D. W. Cartwright, *Regional Employment in Industry, 1940-1970,* Social and Economics Statistics Administration (Washington, D.C.: U.S. Government Printing Office, n.d.)

* Coefficients of variation equals standard deviation of shares (percentages) of employment accounted for by given industry divided by mean of shares in that industry.

one of five SMSAs (21 percent) was a national, regional, or subregional service center (that is, nodal) characterized by relatively large shares of employment in business services. The largest group, however, consisted of SMSAs heavily specialized in manufacturing (30 percent). Three other types of major speciali- zation could be distinguished: government (13 percent), medical- educational (5 percent), and resort (3 percent). A large group of places (27 percent) did not appear to be sufficiently specialized to be classified by major function and were placed in the "mixed" category. Many of these latter places gave evidence of consider- able specialization in certain business service categories but also had relatively large shares of emloyment in some noncentral place activity such as manufacturing.

The nature of a metropolitan area's export activities has important implications. Nodal places may be expected to attract and develop persons with a wide range of white collar skills, including professionals and technicians, whereas nonnodal places will tend to specialize more narrowly in blue collar or service occupations. The nature of the export sector also affects the character of local recreational and cultural institutions. Large nodal places tend to be the home of museums, concert halls, and theaters, all of which are attended and supported by residents of the surrounding area as well as by visitors. Places with more narrowly based export sectors that do not service a particular region have difficulty developing and maintaining such institu- tions. Many places, of course, will have mixed nodal-nonnodal characteristics, but the generalization that the type of economic specialization influences the nature of physical and human re- sources holds, nevertheless.

When SMSAs are analyzed simply in terms of size, larger places tend to show greatest concentrations of employment in business services. This means that larger places are major exporters of such services even though several of the larger places have heavy manufacturing concentrations as well. To an important extent, past growth has proceeded through agglomeration of services; the availability of such services has provided the basis for location of national or regional corporate and institutional head- quarters and major colleges, universities, and cultural establish- ments.

A second observation involves the role played by business services in the places classified as specialized in a single major activity. In most manufacturing places, there appears to be a dearth of business services, indicating that supporting services were either internalized within the business organization or are performed by independent firms located in proximity to some distant corporate headquarters. Recreation-resort places show concentrations of employment in FIRE and retail services and in hotels, restaurants, and recreational services but typically not in such business services as wholesaling. The other specialized places—medical-educational centers and places with especially heavy government employment— do not as a rule have broadly based service sectors.

The mix of SMSAs showed relatively limited change from 1960 to 1970. During the decade, few of the metropolitan areas changed their export specialties. Among the 259 SMSAs in the continental United States, only twenty-one, or 8 percent, changed industrial composition of employment sufficiently to warrant reclassification between 1960 and 1970.

There are two important corollaries to this finding. The first is that places that were already centers of business services in 1960 tended to experience the greatest growth in business services during the following decade. The evidence is shown in table 16, which cross-classifies SMSAs on the basis of shares of employment in mainly business services in 1960 and shares of job increases accounted for by growth in mainly business services from 1960 to 1970.[5] Among the 115 places with higher than average shares of 1960 employment accounted for by business services, 80 (70 percent) also had higher than average shares of job increases accounted for by business services during the decade 1960–1970. On the other hand, among the 144 places with below average shares of 1960 employment in business services, only 44 (30 percent) had higher than average shares of job increases in business services from 1960 to 1970. Moreover, 43 of the 55 nodal places (78 percent) were among the group of SMSAs with above average shares of job increases accounted for by expansion of business services, but only 34 of the 78 manufacturing places (44 percent), 30 of the 71 mixed places (42 percent), 13 of the 34 government places (38 percent), 4 of the 7 resort places (57 percent), and none of the 14 medical-educational places showed above average shares of job increases because of business services growth.

Table 16. Where Job Creation in Mainly Business Services Has Occurred, 259 SMSAs (Percent Shares of Job Increases 1960–70 related to Percent Shares of Total Employment, 1960).

| | | Distribution of 259 SMSAs by Share of Total Employment, Mainly Business Services 1960 | | | | | | |
| | | Below mean* | | | | Above mean* | | | |
		Nodal	Mfg.	Other‡	Total	Nodal	Mfg.	Other‡	Total
Distribution of 259 SMSAs by Shares of Job Increases, 1960–1970, Mainly Business Services	Above mean†	0	24	20	44	43	10	27	80
	Below mean†	0	43	57	100	12	1	22	35

Source: See table 15.

* Mean of shares of total employment accounted for by Mainly Business Services in 1960 is 15 percent.

† Mean of shares of job increases accounted for by Mainly Business Services 1960–70 is 18.02 percent.

‡ Includes SMSAs classified as mixed, resort, medical-educational, government.

Such a finding is precisely what urban growth theory would lead us to expect. Development of specialization has proceeded in terms of both human and physical resources by a process of agglomeration in which services already available attract corporate offices and other administrative units, broadening the market and making still further service growth feasible.

A second corollary of the limited change in the nature of export specialization is the fact that places that were primarily manufacturing centers in 1960 made little progress in shifting their economic base toward business service activities. Manufacturing places with less employment in business services at the beginning of the decade were less likely to attract activities that depend on such services and were, therefore, less likely to gain in business services during the period. Of course, local sector business services have increased virtually everywhere because of changes in consumer banking and credit-using practices and other factors (see below), but such changes have been relatively small in most heavily industrialized places.

Widespread Growth of Local Sector Services

Although there has been little tendency for the relative positions of metropolitan areas as exporters of services to shift within the American urban system, significant change has occurred in local sector employment in virtually all places. The decade of the sixties was one of rising and widely diffused per capita income. With this rise in income came an increased consumer demand everywhere for both private and public local sector services—services found in all sizes and types of urban economies. In addition, consumer demand everywhere has been bolstered by the large flow of government expenditures, especially transfer payments that provide not only the indigent and the unemployed but also the retired with a supporting floor of disposable income. In 1976, these transfer payments accounted for almost 14 percent of total personal income, up from less than 7 percent in 1950, a quarter century earlier.

The health-education and other professional classification (largely nonprofit or public sector services) was the source of the most dramatic employment gains in SMSAs during the fifties and sixties. More than a fifth (22 percent) of all job increases from 1950 to 1960 and nearly a third (33 percent) of job increases from 1960 to 1970 were accounted for by these activities. Expansion was heavily financed out of the public purse at state and federal levels and, accordingly, was not confined to selected locations. Although a few medical and educational centers grew extremely rapidly, medical, educational, and other professional employment expansion was important everywhere. Of the 259 SMSAs within the American economy, in only 12 did the classification account for less than 24 percent of all job increases during the sixties. Similarly, growth in retailing and in most other consumer services occurred everywhere, with at least 10 percent of job increases in

206 SMSAs occurring as a result of expansion of retail employment.

This means that employment growth in industrial categories involved largely in the delivery of consumer services was virtually ubiquitous and, accordingly, has served to enlarge the local sector of almost all metropolitan places. This is true to a significant extent for producer services as well. As noted above, these services belong in both sectors; in part, they provide for the needs of business and government and, in part, for the needs of consumers. For examples of business services as local sector activities, we may look to the FIRE classification. In recent decades, firms within this grouping have come to render an increasing number of services to consumers. The variety of checking, investment, and lending services carried out by banks has become ever more elaborate. At the same time, there has been a sharp rise in the use of consumer installment credit, while savings banks have risen from a trivial status to play a major role among consumer-serving financial institutions. In the insurance field, the types of coverage available to the man on the street have proliferated. All of this means a rise in the extent to which business services are consumer-oriented and are, accordingly, found in almost every city and town.

Thus, local sector growth in services has been large and has occurred in virtually all metropolitan areas. This means that *on the surface*—in terms of types of firms and of new jobs created—all metropolitan places appear to be becoming increasingly alike. But such generalized local sector growth disguises the important fact that producer and consumer services may play strategic roles in the export sector in some places and not in others. It also disguises the fact that the mix of skills required and consequently the types of job opportunities that open up will vary to a considerable degree from one place to another within the urban hierarchy.

Some Evidence of Qualitative Differences among Services: The Advanced Corporate Services

The measures examined above provide evidence of the tendency for producer services to be relatively more important, at least in terms of shares of employment, in larger metropolises than in small and permit us to distinguish those places that are specialized as service centers from those that are not. They do not tell us much, however, about the qualitative aspects of urban specialization in such services; for example, the extent to which high-level expertise in producer services tends to be centered in certain large metropolitan areas.

Robert Cohen's recent work provides considerable insight into the locational characteristics of the *advanced corporate services,* firms that provide highly specialized services to corporate headquarters. Some of his major findings are as follows.

There have been relatively few changes in the rankings of major cities in the location of leading corporate headquarters during recent decades. New York retains its supremacy although it has lost almost forty "Fortune's 500" headquarters over the past twenty years. Chicago continues to rank second. The most notable changes have been the rise of the importance of Los Angeles and Houston and the decline of Pittsburgh. Where changes did occur, they were often related to corporate acquisitions, the acquired companies typically becoming the clients of the new parent's advanced service firms. In this way, such service firms become larger and capable of developing a higher level of expertise. At the same time, the host city strengthens its relative position.

Banking resources and service capabilities are strongly concentrated in a restricted number of large cities. New York banks hold over 31 percent of the nation's deposits; San Francisco is in second place with almost 13 percent. These two may be regarded as both national and regional centers, whereas the other major places, Boston, Atlanta, Dallas, Houston, Minneapolis, Chicago, Seattle, and Los Angeles, function largely as regional banking centers only. Chicago, however, ranks third behind San Francisco in international banking, which is even more highly concentrated. Investment banking activity is the most concentrated of all financial activities and is dominated by New York City.[6]

This centralization of banking works to the distinct advantage of the host cities involved because banking services are closely tied to a variety of other advanced services. Cohen observes:

The ability of banks to offer the extensive international financial services, specialized financial services, and services to major corporations is greatly aided by the agglomeration of other advanced services in the same metropolis. . . . The legal services demanded by banks in formulating complex credit agreements for corporations often necessitate frequent and rapid contact between bank executives and the bank's counsel. . . . Banks also tend to attract financial printers and communications facilities to the metropolis, but perhaps most important in buttressing the strength of a major financial community is the presence of non-bank financial institutions which provide alternative sources of funding for corporate customers.[7]

The legal profession has grown rapidly in the nation's regional centers, with the greatest gains occurring in the largest cities of the burgeoning South and West. The nation's largest law firms (each with a varied staff of specialists) are to be found almost entirely in New York, Chicago, Philadelphia, Washington, Cleveland, and Houston, although Cleveland in the aging industrial belt appears to be losing ground. The most dramatic rise has been in the position of Washington as increasing needs of corporations and trade associations for information regarding regulations and for closer contact with government officials has caused them to seek expert counsel there. In the field of international law, New York holds first place, with Washington and Chicago sharing second and important concentrations in Los Angeles, Houston, San Francisco, Atlanta, and Miami. As noted earlier, the large corporate law firms work closely not only with headquarters, but with banks and accounting firms as well. Law firms dealing with investment banks are highly concentrated in New York.

The spatial distribution of accounting services differs from that of legal and banking services in that the top accounting firms are not located simply in the major cities but operate through a system of branches. Through these branches they are able to serve the day-to-day needs of the numerous installations of their major clients, the large corporations, as well as those of smaller regional and local firms. Headquarters of the top accounting firms (the "big eight") are concentrated in New York, although two are located in Chicago and Cleveland. Accounting has been one of the most rapidly growing of the business services, especially in such favored regional centers as Houston and Atlanta. The more sophisticated accounting services, such as preparation of audits for underwriting, are handled in conjunction with lawyers and bankers in the largest urban centers. In addition, the major accounting firms have increasingly come to perform important roles as consultants for their large corporate clients.

These findings serve principally to make the point that the most advanced corporate services are located in very large urban centers. Yet they also make clear that business services and business firms are interdependent and that there is a hierarchical arrangement in the degree of specialization of services that conforms to the size hierarchy of metropolitan places. What Cohen has done by clarifying the relationship between the most advanced services and major corporate headquarters remains to be accomplished by future research for the lower levels of producer services and for the smaller metropolitan places.

Suburbanization and the Intrametropolitan Distribution of Services

Thus far our discussion of urbanization of the services has ignored intrametropolitan shifts in industries and employment. Yet the entire postwar period has been marked by very rapid growth of suburban areas at the same time that cities have shown markedly less growth and, in some instances, decline and deterioration.

To understand why services have been affected differentially in suburb and city, it is important to underscore several key aspects of the suburbanization process. Suburbanization has been a complex process of shifting both residential and economic functions from city to suburb while at the same time cities were taking on new functions.

The rapid pace of suburbanization has been largely the result of several sets of forces, including the increased importance of automobiles and trucks, coupled with the building of interstate and other major highway arteries connecting city and outlying areas; the modernization of manufacturing plant, requiring more generous use of space; the rise in per capita income, permitting new choices in residence; the search for a more spacious environment, especially for raising children.

Under this combination of circumstances, manufacturing firms found it possible to build single-story suburban plants that were more suitable than the old multistory factories of the city while at the same time finding ready access to the new highway transportation matrix that was rapidly supplanting the railway system in the movement of goods. Simultaneously, middle- and upper-income families shifted residence to suburban areas from whence they could commute readily to jobs within the city or to newly developing employment in the outlying areas.

What is particularly striking is that the rapid growth of the affluent suburban middle class has created a major demand for local sector services (for example, shopping centers, hospitals, schools, and local government activities). Although manufacturing has been an important source of growth in income and employment, the leading edge of employment growth has been in local sector services, principally consumer services such as retailing and local government, but including also activities that are nominally producer services but are purchased in large measure by individuals (lawyers, real estate firms, and the like). Growth in local sector services has been caused in a measure by "import substitution," with the suburbs replacing services previously provided by (that is, imported from) the city's economy.

At the same time, cities have undergone transition. Manufacturing has declined in importance, and local sector services have in many places encountered declines or at least stagnation in demand with the loss of much middle-class patronage. Producer services, however, have expanded within the city, and central business districts have been rebuilt and enlarged. The importance of this development has varied, being relatively important in the nodal cities but less so in the more industrialized ones. The centrality of the central business district, the opportunity it provides for face-to-face interaction among firms and the banks, lawyers, accountants, and other professionals who serve them has in the past favored the central city as a seat for corporate headquarters and for higher level services.

A correlate to the development of producer services within the central city is the development of an infrastructure of supporting

89

services. Jean Gottman has called attention to the importance of restaurants, theater, universities, hotels, specialty shops, and transportation facilities to create both the environment and access necessary for the functioning of what he calls the quarternary services—services that deal in corporate and government transactions and require intensive personal interaction among representatives of corporations, services, and government.[8] He discusses this development of quarternary services principally in terms of the largest cities, but concedes the need to explore the role of lesser cities as well.

New Trends in the Location of Services

In general, a trend toward decentralization has marked the location of corporate activities during the postwar years. In addition to manufacturing plants, corporate headquarters have tended to leave the central city and a variety of "back office" activities have been spun off to outlying areas or to nonmetropolitan places. Increasingly, it is claimed that cities, especially the large, old cities of the East, are crime-ridden, dirty, physically deteriorated, and characterized by high taxes, high wage rates, and a labor supply less well educated than that of the suburbs.

The extent to which there will be further shifts of headquarters and of service activities to the suburbs remains unsettled. One can readily envision two quite different scenarios, each with a large number of variations.

In the first, the suburbs continue to develop, and the focus of activity shifts outward. Institutions that are slow to move, such as hospitals and educational institutions, gravitate bit by bit toward the large, affluent middle-income clientele. The aging of housing stock in some suburban towns and small satellite cities brings about a filtering process resulting in the in-migration of some lower-income families with a consequent broadening of the labor force. At the same time, the concentration of middle- and upper-income residents in the suburbs creates a demand for moving higher level service activities employing professionals and semi-professionals closer to the residences of those who man such firms and institutions. Anything that can be spun off from the city becomes a candidate for suburbanization. Moreover, with growth, suburban markets broaden, and interaction and mutual attraction among various producers and consumer services begins. One or more of the larger satellite cities (such as Stamford, Connecticut, in the greater New York City area) may become the nucleus around which significant concentrations of office activity and services develop.

Meanwhile, the central city increasingly is victimized by the economics of heavy overhead costs. Its burden of public sector services declines only slightly, but its tax base suffers deep erosion. Congestion is not relieved significantly as the pace of economic activity slackens, for the transportation system becomes increasingly outmoded. Environmentally and economically the city is perceived as an inferior place to live or do business. In the end it must fall back upon a policy of retrenchment and reliance upon infusions of cash from higher levels of government.

In the second scenario, the city effects a transformation and remains viable, while the suburbs continue to play a symbiotic role within the overall metropolitan economy—giving to and taking from the central city.[9] For such a scenario to obtain, the central city must remain an economically superior location for at least part of its traditional functions. It would seem apparent that the central city no longer offers the lowest cost location for most manufacturers, especially those requiring extensive use of land. Its advantage lies principally in its centrality within the metropolitan market and the physical arrangement that makes it possible at once to draw readily upon a large labor market and to host a variety of firms and activities that function most effectively near each other.

Producer, government, and very specialized consumer services must constitute the major economic base (although selected specialty manufacturers may also find a city location desirable). From what we have seen of the tendency for certain cities to become specialized both in their physical facilities and labor markets, it seems likely that those already performing as service centers will stand the greatest chance of success in effecting this transformation.

A recent study of corporate moveouts in New York City revealed that although a significant number of large corporate

91

headquarters have moved out of the city (largely to the suburbs) they have continued to use central city advanced services.[10] Moreover, because of its increased importance as a national and international center, the city has increased its service complex to the point that utilization of office space has grown and service employment has increased.

Certain major social trends are at work providing important opportunities for economic renaissance of the central city. One involves the increasing insistence of women for opportunities not simply in traditionally "female labeled" jobs but alongside men in managerial, professional, and technical positions in corporate offices in the advanced corporate services and in universities and medical centers. Typically, there are more well-paying jobs for women in the city, jobs that are likely to be more accessible than in the spatially more dispersed economy of the suburbs. Moreover, if there are no children or if childbearing is postponed and the number of offspring is limited (as is increasingly the case), the city becomes more attractive as a place to reside than formerly, the suburb, perhaps less so. Certain conditions, however, must be met: provision for adequate housing and improvement of the city's environment in personal safety, levels of pollution, general cleanliness, and ease of getting around.

Wilbur Thompson has argued that "unloading" of residents from the crumbling and dysfunctional areas of the inner city is essential for its renewal.[11] His view is essentially optimistic: if, through the outward filtering of housing and the migration process, the decaying areas of the inner city can be cleared away and modernized, the city will find a new stability. There are significant social costs inherent in such filtering, for many of the poor are likely to be uprooted. If filtering can be accompanied by improved opportunities for jobs, then such social costs will be substantially offset.

There is already solid evidence that important first steps are being taken in a number of American cities toward rehabilitation of inner-city housing. In Atlanta, Inman Park, a large and formerly popular residential area that had become degraded to slum levels, has now been largely reclaimed by young middle-income couples. Similar successes have been scored in New York City (Brooklyn

92

Heights) and Washington, D.C. (Capitol Hill), as well as in Philadelphia and San Francisco.

It is significant that many of these renovations were accomplished without public sector sponsorship and in the face of major financial obstacles arising out of the unwillingness of the banking community to provide credit. If, as appears likely, an important new trend is under way in many of our older cities, new initiatives by the public sector could go far toward expediting the renaissance of middle-class inner-city housing.

Restoration of middle-class neighborhoods will tend to bring about improved security and levels of cleanliness, particularly when such restoration is accompanied by formation of strong neighborhood associations that both foster a sense of individual responsibility and give rise to aggressive group efforts to exert pressure on city government. In addition, new public awareness of the need for pollution control and improved transportation coupled with new federal programs to assist financing and otherwise expedite such changes promise significant advances in the years immediately ahead.

The Spatial Distribution of Occupations and Skills

Thus far I have distinguished between local sector and export sector activity, examined the hierarchical nature of the system of metropolitan places and of export services, and taken note of new trends in the location of services. The implications of this analysis for the spatial distribution of occupations and skills need to be examined. At one level, the translation from industrial composition to the occupational composition of the work force is simple. The similarity of local sector services in different places means a similarity of jobs required in delivering local sector services everywhere, but such jobs will not necessarily be identical. Large places will require more elaborate organization with higher levels of administration and more specialized staffs. Thus, in metropolitan places, large and small, retail clerks, policemen, school teachers, postal mail handlers, service station attendants, and auto mechanics will be employed, but larger places are likely to employ relatively more specialists. Moreover, to the extent that the most specialized export producer services, public sector services, and cultural, health, and educational services are found in very large service centers, the most skilled and highly trained professionals will work in these places, although, as we have seen, there will also be much larger numbers of workers with lesser skills, earning much lower incomes, in these organizations. The general conclusion is that within the largest central places one finds the broadest range of service activities and of occupational requirements. Moreover, the largest places, where markets are broadest, will offer the widest range of opportunities for employment of special skills. At lower levels of the urban hierarchy, both the highest level of specialization and the variety of activities will be more restricted with corresponding restriction upon the range of career opportunities. Finally, in specialized places (such as manufacturing and government cities) there may be some demand for high orders of specialization, but the range of activities is likely to be restricted.

But what are the locational implications of the changes in occupational composition that were noted in Chapter 4? What does it mean when there are shifts in the relative importance of various occupations such as declines in numbers of salespersons and increases in numbers of clerical workers?

We have little evidence based on careful research, but it is not unlikely that where productivity has increased through rearrangement of work the effect is to shift work from the operational to the administrative unit. Thus, reduction in numbers of salespersons at retail chain outlets through standardization of merchandising procedures and computerization may result in an increased number of managerial and clerical personnel, but this change is likely to occur at an administrative center located in an entirely different area. The shift may augment employment in the firm's headquarters operation or, quite as likely if the firm is large, it may give rise to new jobs in an administrative office separate from the headquarters organization.

It would be a mistake, however, to stress excessively the relationship between services and central city growth. Many services, or at least certain functions of service organizations, are in large measure footloose in terms of location. Where scale is large, functions such as billing and auditing (for example, the auditing offices of the Internal Revenue Service) can be relegated to organizations located in suburban and nonmetropolitan places. Under such conditions the growth of services gives rise to new locational requirements that can be met through a variety of alternative arrangements.

Conclusions

Metropolitan places may be regarded as economies that export, import, and provide local sector activities to serve the needs of residents. Services as well as goods may comprise the export sector. Indeed, for many cities and towns (though not for all), the provision of services to outside markets, frequently to corporate headquarters or other administrative units, is the principal export function. Moreover, there is a heirarchy of such export services based on economies of scale and market size, which means that a few very large, metropolitan service centers will host the most highly specialized services in addition to a variety of less specialized ones; a larger number of medium-sized places will offer a somewhat narrower array of services, few of which will be as highly specialized; and a still larger number of smaller places will provide immediate hinterlands with an even more restricted group of services. In addition, some metropolitan places do not function as general service centers. Instead they are principally involved in exporting manufactures or in hosting some very specialized group of activities (for example, resort or government centers).

On the other hand, strictly local sector services, those that provide for everyday needs, will be found close at hand wherever men and women reside. The volume of such services rendered is related to numbers of residents and to levels of disposable income.

Thus we see that a considerable number of local sector services (retailing, local government, churches, public schools and community colleges, smaller health institutions, movie houses, and so forth) will be virtually ubiquitous, while export-linked service activities will be found only in selected places with the largest providing the most specialized and complex group of services.

Such a simplified categorization of services helps to make clear the kinds of problems faced by metropolitan places today. As employment in goods production has stabilized, declined, or shifted geographically, communities must look to services to provide increased employment. To an important extent, such increases have occurred everywhere through expansion of local sector services stemming from the expansion of the not-for-profit sector (for example, increases in health, education, and government services) and from a general increase in per capita income.

But in export sector services, expansion has been selective. In business services, places already specialized as service centers have tended to show the best rates of employment growth. Certain government centers and resort centers have also experienced above average growth. In general, metropolitan areas in regions favored by growth have fared best. Metropolitan places specialized in goods production located in mature, low-growth areas appear to be facing the greatest problems of transforming economies to viable service export bases. Thus, as metropolitan areas increasingly stand in competition for service employment, some places appear to enjoy distinct advantages over others.

But there exists yet another spatial dimension to the growth of services: intrametropolitan changes are occurring, as well as shifts from metropolitan to nonmetropolitan areas. Not only has employment in goods production been transferred to suburban and to nonmetropolitan areas, but local sector activities have followed population shifts. Although producer services and a variety of other supporting services have shown a strong attachment to the central city, a complex process of adjustment is at work in which some services are being drawn away from the city and some are not. Just how the central city will fare ultimately is probably not foreordained, but, rather, may be significantly influenced by public policy. In spite of a variety of difficult and in some instances seemingly intractable problems, there are a number of strong social forces at work favoring a revitalization of the inner city. In selected cities, there is already evidence of a transformation in progress toward revitalization of the central city through initiatives both within and outside the public sector.

6

Growth of Services and the Outlook for Employment: Issues for Study

In the opening chapter, four general conclusions were set forth. The first related to the demand linkages and possibilities for substitution that have caused levels of output (though not of employment) of goods and services to expand at roughly similar rates.

A second related to productivity. New forces at work promise significant productivity gains in services arising out of new managerial approaches to the organization of service firms and institutions, made possible in part by greater opportunities for large-scale operation and application of modern technology. Productivity differentials are likely to remain, however, especially in the public sector, where signals from the market economy for changes in resource allocation and managerial improvement are largely missing.

The third general conclusion was that the service work force is not, on average, better paid or more highly skilled than the nonservice work force. Although at the upper levels there are highly paid, skilled professionals and executives, the service work force is characterized by a larger proportion of workers at the lower end of the earnings scale, by a higher proportion of women and minority workers, by higher percentages of part-time employment, and by fewer structural and institutional arrangements that enhance job security. Moreover, the evidence of postwar experience does not point to a generalized trend toward an upward redistribution of service jobs, even though growth in services has tended to bring about some upgrading of female employment from traditionally low levels.

Finally, it is important to examine the composition and growth of employment in services within an urban framework. Services tend to be classifiable as local sector, which are relatively ubiquitous, and export sector, which vary among places by type and level of specialization. Metropolitan places may be seen as parts of a hierarchical urban system that in large measure determines the location of a number of major types of service activities and employment.

These general conclusions give rise to several important questions—actually, issues, for they are questions of major importance. The first concerns the magnitudes of two sets of opposing forces—those that act to curtail service employment and those that act to increase it. A second set, closely related, pertains to the kind of jobs that are being created and how access is to be determined, while a third involves the problems arising as service sector growth brings relocation of jobs. Finally, a fourth set concerns the difficulties encountered in shifting from goods to service employment under conditions of low rates of economic growth.

The Postindustrial Society

Before examining these issues, I must call attention to a concept that in recent years has been widely associated with the growth of services: the concept of the "postindustrial society." Though often used as a convenient catch phrase indicating no more than an awareness that we are living in a period in which occupational and industrial structures have changed markedly, the term was intended by its originator, sociologist Daniel Bell, to identify a theory of social development. Although it is not an objective of this monograph to provide a critique of Bell's provocative theory, it would be remiss to fail to recognize the degree to which it is concerned with the growth of services and the general lines of development that are visualized.

Although Bell states explicitly that the centrality of the service sector and its expansion should not be conceived as his major thesis, his description of the rise of the services and of the increasing significance of certain occupations, found largely within the services, plays a major part in his argument.[1] At the outset, he specifies five dimensions, or components, that distinguish the postindustrial society: (1) economic sector: the change from a goods-producing to a service economy; (2) occupational distribution: the preeminence of the professional and technical class; (3) axial principle (that is, the principle that most importantly characterizes the society): the centrality of theoretical knowledge as the source of innovation and of policy formation for the society; (4) future orientation: the control of technology and technological assessment; and (5) decision making: the creation of a new "intellectual technology."[2]

Thus, Bell's work differs from the present analysis in its long-range perspective, its emphasis on the shifting importance of certain classes within society, and its delineation of the probable lines along which social conflict is likely to develop. Bell does, however, treat briefly a number of the points that have been examined in the present study. He recognizes the parallel development of goods and services where services and servicelike activities have been "auxiliary" to industrial development or essential to the distribution of mass consumption goods (for example, transportation, utilities, wholesale and retail trade, finance, insurance), but does not explore the extent to which goods-services demand complementarities in consumer behavior or in government and other not-for-profit activities may continue to obtain in the years ahead.[3] He calls attention to productivity and price differentials that lead to substitution and economizing and act to constrain the expansion of services, especially in the public sector but, curiously, makes no effort to explain how these constraints will be overcome as the postindustrial society moves increasingly toward a service orientation.[4] Finally, he presents evidence of the rising importance of women in the service work force and the expansion of low-end service jobs (garage workers, hotel and restaurant workers, and the like), but emphasizes only the continued expansion of employment in service jobs requiring a high level of expertise.[5]

Work such as Bell's is useful in providing constructs with which we may seek to discern the general directions in which social evolution is taking us. Yet social and economic development are not likely to move along any direct course but rather to demonstrate a variety of twists and turns before the long-run outcome becomes apparent. The purpose of the present study has been to examine the nature of service sector growth within this shorter time frame and to point up certain issues that are likely to be of key importance in the years immediately ahead.

Forces Acting to Alter the Size of the Service Work Force

Among the issues relating to changes in the demand for service workers, three stand out as being both of critical importance and in need of additional study: (1) Will technology reduce the demand for white collar workers? (2) What are the prospects for growth in public sector employment? (3) Does self-employment offer a major area of opportunity for additional service jobs?

Technology and the Reduction of White Collar Employment

It was observed in Chapter 4 that the increase in clerical jobs has been a major source of service sector employment expansion but that there was reason to expect efforts to be exerted to reduce such employment or at least to resist expansion. Both cost considerations and the state of technology indicate the importance of the latter. Office costs, once a matter of relatively little concern, have burgeoned until they now comprise a major item of organizational expense. Alan Purchase, senior industrial economist at Stanford Research Institute, has stated that "where office costs used to be 20% to 30% of the total in a company they have now grown to 40% to 50% of all costs."[6] IBM spokesmen maintained in 1975 that the average secretary's salary was 68 percent higher and the cost of turning out a business letter 40 percent greater than ten years previously.[7]

In the face of such cost increases, the development of new technology combining the capabilities of telephone, television, computer, and xerographic processes offers major opportunities for cost saving and improved performance of clerical and other white collar personnel in both service and nonservice organizations. For example, the U.S. Post Office Department reported in 1976 that business communications costs were sharply lower when new techniques were employed than when conventional mail was used:

Tie-line network call	$ .74/6 minutes
WATS line	$1.10/6 minutes
Facsimile process	$1.97/6 minute page
Teletype	$2.42/66 words
U.S. mail letter	$6.41 page[8]

Evidence drawn from specific case histories strongly supports the case for modern technology in reducing costs: (1) One public utility that has installed a central word processing system saved more than $200,000 in labor in the first year and anticipated a saving of more than a million dollars a year when the full program was brought into operation.[9] (2) An electronic mail system installed to operate during off-peak hours of a private telephone system saved one manufacturer $200,000 on postage for intra-company mail.[10] (3) The Navy Recruiting Command's word processing system links 198 automatic typewriters and 150 dictation units at 78 locations with headquarters located at Arlington, Virginia. It cost $1.5 million, but at the time of installation, it was expected to save more than $4.6 million each year, largely by eliminating additions to manpower.[11]

But these are only isolated examples. The new technology is already widely used in businesses, nonprofit institutions, and government. Its known capabilities, broad opportunities for application, and declining relative costs have prompted estimates of high rates of adoption. A leading Xerox Corporation research executive has stated, "There is absolutely no question that there will be a revolution in the office in the next 20 years. What we are doing will change the office like the jet plane revolutionized travel and the way TV has altered family life."[12] Vincent E. Guiliano of Arthur D. Little, Inc., a major auditing and consulting firm, estimates that the use of paper in business for records and correspondence should be declining by 1980 and that, "by 1990, most record-handling will be electronic."[13]

There are, however, certain obstacles to a rapid transition to the new technology. Adoption typically involves considerable reorganization of office work assignments, physical layout, and administrative organization. Not surprisingly, there has been resistance to these necessary rearrangements of work processes. Moreover, their application is likely to be more successful in large organizations than small, although declining costs of hardware and improvement in procedures increasingly put the new technology within the reach of at least medium-sized organizations.

For many applications, of course, the new technology is already well established, involving communications, administrative controls, filing, inventory controls, billing, and a variety of other functions in offices, warehouses, hospitals, government installations, airlines, motels, and a wide variety of other activities. That such a highly significant development is widespread is not at issue. The issue is the rate at which it is likely to proceed in the years ahead and its probable employment impact. Thus far there seems to have been little observable effect in the form of reduced employment, although examples can be cited. Typically, new equipment and work arrangements are utilized to permit the organization to handle a larger volume of work, to provide new and improved services, and to increase managerial efficiency. Creation of new jobs has, doubtless, been sharply reduced relative to what it would have otherwise been, but the magnitude of this effect is virtually impossible to measure. It is clear, however, that over time the adoption of the new technology must act to curtail employment opportunities unless there are strong expansionary forces elsewhere within the economy. How rapidly this will occur, how large will be its impact, and what jobs will be affected, we do not know.

Thus, our lack of any clear understanding of the probable impact of the new technology in terms of demand for labor stands as a major issue deserving of special study.

Reductions in Public Sector Expenditures

As this is written, many sections of the country are caught up in a storm of protest over the level of public spending and taxation.

Not only has the much discussed Jarvis-Gann Amendment rolled back property taxes in California by roughly 57 percent, but the state of Colorado has put into force five new laws that will lighten the burden of taxes on most residents this year.[14] Significant economies within state governments are already in force with surpluses of more than $33 billion reported for 1977.[15]

Not only is the demand for such reductions in taxes and expenditures widespread at the state government level, but it is also widely voiced by individuals and the press as it relates to municipal and federal government. Since expansion in government at all levels has been a major source of job creation in services in the postwar period, we are faced here, as in the case of increasing application of new technology, with a development that may significantly alter new job opportunities. Yet once again, we have little understanding of the extent of the employment impact of such developments.

Possible Employment Growth through Increases in Small Service Firms

In 1965, Victor Fuchs called attention to the important role of small firms within the services and suggested that the growth of services would act to increase the opportunities for growth of small firms within the economy, resulting in greater opportunities for self-employment and more congenial work arrangements, but presenting at the same time problems in bringing about productivity improvements.[16]

Fuchs's argument rested on the observation that a larger proportion of organizations in service than in nonservice activities were small and that such a tendency was likely to persist as service employment grows in relative importance. The most recent estimates indicate that the tendency still holds, but there are difficulties in interpreting trends and some serious reasons to question Fuchs's generally optimistic conclusions.

Table 17 shows that a much higher percentage of service employment continues to be found in small and medium-sized establishments (fewer than twenty and twenty to five hundred employees) in service activities than in manufacturing, although during the period 1962 to 1975 the share of employment in small establishments declined in service categories except wholesaling, while rising in medium-sized establishments.

When the distribution of firms for the year 1972 is examined, however, and shorter term trends are assessed, the picture is more ambiguous. The relative importance of small firms fell sharply in all service categories from 1962 to 1972 but increased in all but eating-drinking establishments and selected services from 1972 to 1975. The relative importance of medium-sized firms increased during the 1962–72 period in all services, but declined significantly in wholesaling and slightly in selected services and FIRE during the most recent years. Just why reversals of trends in size of service establishments have occurred recently and whether or not such developments can be projected is not at all clear.

Moreover, a serious problem of interpretation arises regarding definition of an "establishment," the reporting unit from which the data are derived. These units may be independent firms, branches of large corporate entities, or franchised outlets. Such heterogenity poses difficulties in analysis because opportunities for self-employment and development of individual initiative are not likely to be the same in branches or franchised outlets as in independent firms of the same size.

Thus, once again we are sorely in need of better knowledge of what changes have taken place and what may be expected. General observation would seem to indicate that the small independent firm is not gaining in relative terms in such activities as retailing, auto repair, auto rentals, accounting, or the delivery of health services. Across a broad spectrum of service activities, one notes the tendency for branches of large firms or franchised outlets to preempt business opportunities in choice locations and in the most lucrative types of services. It is by no means clear that the new service economy will be marked by a large number of attractive new opportunities for individual initiative.

This is not to say, however, that small service operations will not proliferate. Services are the last frontier for small independent enterprise. Small boutiques, specialty shops, and the like will, no doubt, continue to open up, especially if employment opportunities diminish elsewhere. But mortality rates for such enterprises are high, and returns on those that survive tend to be pitiably low.

Table 17. Percentage of Employment within Small and Medium-Sized Establishments, for Manufacturing and Categories of Service.

	1962		1972		1975	
	Fewer than 20 employees	20-500 employees	Fewer than 20 employees	20-500 employees	Fewer than 20 employees	20-500 employees
Manufacturing	7	49	6	52	7	51
Wholesale	39	56	34	60	40	55
Retail	49	39	39	47	44	50
Eating-drinking	56	41	40	57	40	59
All other	47	38	39	44	45	48
Selected services†	40	43	33	46	33	45
FIRE	33	45	28	48	31	46

Source: U.S. Bureau of the Census, *County Business Patterns, 1962, 1972,* and *1975* (Washington, D.C.: Government Printing Office, 1964, 1974, and 1977).

* Percentages of employment in establishments with more than 500 employees are not shown.
† Include hotels and other lodging places; personal services, miscellaneous business services; auto repair, services, and garages; miscellaneous repair services; motion pictures; amusement and recreation services; medical and other health services; legal services and miscellaneous services.

Kinds of Jobs and the Problem of Access

A major issue relating to growth in service employment is the quality of jobs that are opening up. Is the service sector being upgraded? Are new problems of access to jobs being created for minorities and other groups currently experiencing high rates of unemployment?

Both Fuchs and Bell have emphasized the increasing role to be played by professionals and skilled technicians as we move further toward a service-oriented economy. Yet the evidence presented in Chapter 4 has shown that many jobs in the broad professional-technical occupational category are neither highly skilled nor especially well paid. Further, there has been rapid growth in low-paid clerical and sales personnel and in the so-called service worker category. What then is the dominant trend?

Clearly, this is a major issue. Introduction of new technology typically involves substantial investment in costly equipment. Fuchs has argued that to a significant extent there is also a substantial element of "labor embodiment" in technological change in the services, meaning that there is also increased investment in the training of individuals.[17] This would seem to be the case in health services and in many educational and public sector services. Discussions of the new office technology in the technical literature indicate that a major objective is to increase the level of proficiency and responsibility of secretaries, permitting them to function in roles leading to subsequent promotion to executive status.

Yet at the same time, the tasks of salespersons are frequently rendered more routine by computerized procedures, and in a variety of jobs involving janitorial cleaning, delivery of goods, and ordinary maintenance there is little evidence pointing to significant upgrading.

It is entirely possible, though the case is by no means proven, that we are moving toward a sharply dichotomized service work force offering, on one hand, the skilled, responsible, and relatively well-paying jobs of certain professionals, trained technicians, or artisans, but on the other, the unskilled, undemanding, and poorly paid jobs of salespersons, service workers, or laborers.

If such is the case, we face major problems of equity within our society. Upward mobility is an essential characteristic of a democratic society, requiring access to preferred employment for those with native talent and the willingness to work for promotion through the ranks of the hierarchy. Where the labor market is sharply dichotomized—where a middle tier of jobs is missing— access to the upper level of jobs is extremely difficult for those denied the education and special training necessary for advancement.

Relocation of Jobs and Problems of Spatial Adjustment

The analysis in Chapter 5 has shown how the basic function of services differ within the metropolitan economy, some being residentiary in nature (that is, local sector) and thus essentially ubiquitous, while others are export-oriented and thus spatially specialized. It has shown, further, that the degree of specialization in services varies among places, tending to be highest in large regional and national service centers. Finally, it has shown that when manufacturing activity tends to be located in outlying areas, either suburban or nonmetropolitan, cities are increasingly dependent upon services to provide employment, although all places are not equally endowed in competing for such jobs.

But patterns of location of services are by no means established. The new technology in intraorganizational communication, record keeping, and managerial controls emphasizes the use of centralized and shared computer facilities, serving a variety of corporate or government functions. Such technology creates, in theory at least, the opportunity to separate functions spatially while maintaining centralized control. What we know of locational policies of large corporations indicates that headquarters functions tend to be performed in large metropolitan areas, usually but not always in large cities and in proximity to advanced corporate services. But how flexible corporations or public sector organizations can afford to be in locating back office, research, warehousing, and lower echelon administrative units is something we know little or nothing about.

Thus we do not have as yet any clear understanding of how the location of service employment is likely to evolve or of the degree of latitude that exists within the system in bringing jobs into areas where unemployment experience is unsatisfactory. Clearly, this is an area in which research is needed.

Problems of Shifting from Goods to Service Employment under Conditions of Low Growth Rates

In recent years it has been taken almost as an article of faith that we may project the past into the future. Because we have shifted steadily from goods to services employment without major dislocations (though surely not without a number of difficulties and inequities), it is assumed that we will continue to do so. Yet past growth in service employment has been underwritten in large measure by the growth in the demand for health, education, and public sector services, all of which give considerable evidence of entering into a period of sharply reduced rates of expansion. How, then, if productivity continues to advance more rapidly in goods than in services, is the economy to generate sufficient additional service jobs to assure full employment?

The issue is very closely related to the overall growth performance of the economy in several ways. The first relates to the basic tendencies toward complementarity of demand and possibilities for substitution between goods and services. Where growth of service employment reflects largely productivity differentials, the cost of services relative to goods tends to rise. Under conditions of low levels of growth in aggregate demand, growth in service employment is fraught with difficulties. With little growth in the consumption of goods, there is likely to be little increase in the demand for related services. Moreover, the increasing relative costs of services encourages substitution. In the public sector, any increase in the level of relatively costly services tends to increase taxes and lower disposable income. Taxpayer resistance follows. Except where special needs dictate, as in the case of health services or defense, it is only under conditions of fairly vigorous growth in per capita national income stemming from higher levels of investment and exports that either the consumer or voter is likely to accept easily a substantial shift toward service employment.

To this must be added the problems of spatial adjustment discussed above. The growth of services has tended to be accompanied by an increase in specialization both in firms and personnel and in location. At the same time, new patterns of location have developed in goods production. Thus, a rise in the importance of service employment carries with it the need for spatial readjustment.

Such adjustment is accomplished with relatively little stress when aggregate demand for labor is growing. Employment levels remain relatively high in areas least favored, while in areas where shortages develop demand is met by upgrading, by migration, and by utilizing personnel who might otherwise have left or never entered the labor market. When aggregate demand grows slowly, adjustment is difficult and unemployment is likely to be high—not simply because of the aggregate level of employment demand but because of the imperfections within the system of labor markets.

It is hardly necessary to add that such maladjustments are likely to take their toll disproportionately on those who are least skilled, least experienced, and least able to make difficult adjustments through migration or retraining. These typically are the young, the old, and members of minorities who as a group lack the training and cultural acclimatization to equip them adequately for jobs that are opening up.

Thus growth appears as an essential precondition to a ready and equitable adjustment to substantial shifts from goods to service employment. Yet growth has been relatively slow in recent years, and the prospects for the years ahead are not highly optimistic. Accordingly, the challenge of adjustment to the growth in service employment bids fair to be a difficult one requiring new knowledge and new policies relating to training, recruitment, migration, and regional and urban development.

It is, of course, possible that in the future there will be renewed demands for goods production related to special requirements for energy, housing, or the rebuilding of outmoded capital stock and urban centers. Such conditions would generate new and different demands for services. Regarding such matters, however, we have yet to turn our thoughts and our energies.

Appendix

Marcia Freedman's study *Labor Markets: Segments and Shelters* provides materials appropriate for highlighting certain important characteristics of service employment. Utilizing micro-data from the one in one thousand sample of the census of population and other materials, Freedman has assembled for the year 1970 a 270-cell occupation-industry matrix with matching data for annual earnings and a variety of structural and demographic characteristics including:

> *Structural*
> Percentage with full-time, full-year employment
> Class of worker (percentages wage or salary, government, and self-employed)
> Internal labor market
> Establishment size
> Licensing and accreditation
> Collective bargaining coverage
>
> *Demographic-educational*
> Sex (percent female)
> Education
> Age (percent under twenty-five years)
> Race (percent nonwhite)

Of particular importance for the analysis is the fact that the detailed occupations of the census and industry classifications are aggregated in such a way as to provide groups that are more homogeneous and descriptive than the conventional census categories. Instead of a single category, professional, technical, and kindred services, the component occupations are grouped under two headings: professionals and semiprofessionals-technicians. Instead of the single category, clericals, two headings, office clericals and nonoffice clericals, are formed. Similarly, several new industrial groups are constructed. Retailing is divided into durable retailing and nondurable retailing, and two new service groups, producer services and other consumer services, are formed. The former is based on Harry Greenfield's study *Manpower and the Growth of Producer Services*; the latter consists of a number of clearly defined consumer services that do not fall within the well-defined groups: restaurants-hotels-motels, health services, and education-welfare-nonprofit services, which are among the other industry groups utilized in the matrix.

In order to group these cells into labor market segments, she makes use of a statistical procedure, automatic interaction detector (AID) that tests the structural variables listed above to break out the clusters that are most homogeneous.[1] Upon completion of the analysis, the cells fall into fourteen groups (Table 18), representing labor market segments within which variance in the average annual earnings of component cells is minimized.

A word of caution is in order regarding the earnings measures. The fourteen labor market segments have been ranked according to mean annual earnings and provide a basis for examining income characteristics in the analysis that follows. It should be noted that although the analysis employed in breaking out these segments has sharply reduced variance in earnings among component occupation-industry cells, it has not eliminated it. Not all of the individual cells in, say, segment 9 show annual earnings below those of all cells in segment 8 or above cells in segment 10, although most do. There is some overlap, albeit a relatively small amount. Accordingly, the findings regarding earnings levels, which are based on mean annual earnings for segments, must be looked upon as generalizations and may be subject to some error when subgroups are examined.

In addition, it must be recognized that the analysis is based on sample data. For this reason, certain of the smaller cells are subject to sampling error.

Table 18. Labor Markets Segments, 1970, Selected Information.

Segment Rank	Share of Total Employment (%)	Mean Earnings (all subgroups) ($)	Ratio to Grand Mean	Service Employment (%)
High				
1	2.1	15,794	2.43	77.4
2	5.1	12,484	1.92	35.3
3	3.1	11,280	1.73	60.0
4	1.7	10,087	1.55	53.6
5	2.4	9,861	1.52	47.1
6	6.5	8,759	1.35	37.1
Medium				
7	10.3	7,555	1.16	60.1
8	4.9	7,155	1.10	65.6
9	10.3	6,987	1.07	59.8
10	7.6	6,350	0.98	0
Low				
11	6.6	5,102	0.78	69.3
12	14.7	4,932	0.76	27.7
13	13.6	3,764	0.58	87.4
14	11.2	2,779	0.43	96.8
Total	100.0	6,505	1.00	56.5

Source: Marcia Freedman, *Labor Markets: Segments and Shelters* (Montclair, N.J.: Allanheld, Osmun, 1976), pp. 21, 181–85.

Notes

Chapter 1

1. Victor R. Fuchs, *The Service Industries and U.S. Economic Growth since World War II*, NBER Working Paper No. 211 (Stanford, Calif.: National Bureau of Economic Research, Inc., 1977), p. 4.

2. Important exceptions are George Stigler, *Trends in Employment in the Service Industries* (Princeton, N.J.: Princeton University Press, 1956), Harry I. Greenfield, *Manpower and the Growth of Producer Services* (New York: Columbia University Press, 1966), and Victor R. Fuchs, *The Service Economy* (New York: Columbia University Press, 1968).

3. Fuchs, *The Service Industries and U.S. Economic Growth*, p. 5.

4. This definition follows the practice of Victor Fuchs. See Fuchs, *The Service Economy*, p. 2.

Chapter 2

1. Stefan B. Linder, *The Harried Leisure Class* (New York: Columbia University Press, 1970).

2. Ibid., p. 136.

3. Ibid., p. 51.

4. Harry I. Greenfield, *Manpower and the Growth of Producer Services* (New York: Columbia University Press, 1966), pp. 37–47.

5. Robert Cohen, "The Modern Corporation and the City" (unpublished), Chapters 3 and 4.

6. Eli Ginzberg, "The Pluralistic Economy of the U.S.," *Scientific American*, December 1976, p. 27.

7. Ibid.

8. Eli Ginzberg, "Investments in Health Manpower, A Possible Alternative," in Gordon K. MacLeod and Mark Perlman, eds., *Health Care Capital: Competi-*

tion and Control, Proceedings of the Capital Investment Conference (Pittsburgh, Pa.: University of Pittsburgh Graduate School of Public Health, 1977).

9. National Center for Education Statistics, *Digest of Education Statistics, 1977–78* (Washington, D.C.: U.S. Government Printing Office, 1978), p. 35; and National Center for Education Statistics, *Projections of Education Statistics to 1983–84* (Washington, D.C.: U.S. Government Printing Office, 1975), p. 159.

10. Eli Ginzberg, "How Much Will U.S. Medicine Change in the Decade Ahead?" *Annals of Internal Medicine* 89 (1978): 557–64.

Chapter 3

1. William J. Baumol, "Macroeconomics of Unbalanced Growth: The Anatomy of Urban Crisis," *American Economic Review*, June 1967, pp. 415–26.

2. Ibid., pp. 423–24.

3. Theodore Leavitt, "Management and the 'Post Industrial' Society," *Public Interest*, no. 44 (Summer 1976), pp. 69 ff.

4. Ibid., p. 73.

5. Ibid., pp. 73–74.

6. Ibid., p. 92.

7. Ibid., p. 86.

8. U.S. Department of Commerce, Domestic and International Business Administration, *Service Industries, Trends and Prospects* (Washington, D.C.: U.S.Government Printing Office, 1975), p. 11.

9. Ibid., p. 10.

10. See Chapter 6 for a discussion of trends relating to small firms in services.

11. For an excellent review of the problems of measuring productivity, especially in the public sector, see John P. Ross and Jesse Burkhead, *Productivity in the Local Government Sector* (Lexington, Mass.: D. C. Heath and Co., 1974), Chapter 2.

12. Victor R. Fuchs, *The Service Industries and U.S. Economic Growth since World War II*, NBER Working Paper No. 211 (Stanford, Calif.: National Bureau of Economic Research, Inc., 1977), p. 21. Fuchs, however, does not feel that errors in estimation account for productivity differentials between goods (industry) and services.

13. Robert J. Mowitz, "Some Problems in Dealing with Government Productivity," *Tax Review* 37, no. 8 (1976): 29–32. Mowitz is, of course, not the only student of public sector issues who has dealt with problems and possible approaches relating to productivity in government. Cf. Frederick O'R. Hayes, *Productivity in Local Government* (Lexington, Mass.: D. C. Heath and Co., 1977), pp. 9–17; Ross and Burkhead, *Productivity in the Local Government Sector*, especially Chapter 7.

14. Mowitz, "Problems," pp. 30–31.

15. Ibid., p. 32.

16. Baumol, "Macroeconomics," p. 421.

Chapter 4

1. The analysis of the service work force in this section is based on materials developed by Marcia Freedman in *Labor Markets: Segments and Shelters*

(Montclair, N.J.: Allanheld, Osmun, 1976). Working from a detailed occupation-industry classification of total U.S. employment in 1970, Freedman tested a number of structural variables in order to divide the work force into fourteen segments within which variance in average earnings among component occupation-industry subgroups is minimized. (See Appendix for a brief description of her research.) Table 18 in the Appendix presents information relating to average earnings, principal subgroups (service and nonservice), and percentage of service employment in each of the fourteen segments.

2. The service worker classification identifies a wide-ranging group including such occupations as janitors, bartenders, waiters, dental assistants, practical nurses, airline stewardesses, hairdressers, elevator operators, firemen, policemen, and cooks.

3. The low percentage FT, FY for professionals in the medium-income grouping is in part an artifact of the part-year working arrangements of educational institutions.

4. Freedman, *Labor Markets*, p. 23.

5. Ibid., p. 27.

6. There is reason to believe, however, that for at least some of these groups the share of self-employed and level of subgroup earnings are overestimated. Individuals with losses (negative earnings) were excluded from the analysis and thus from the data utilized. Since only the self-employed may experience losses, such an exclusion acts to reduce the numbers of self-employed and to raise the level of average earnings of the subgroups in which these missing individuals would have been classified. Such an error is likely to be greatest where failure rates are known to be highest, notably among owner-managers in such activities as nondurable retailing, restaurants, and a variety of small consumer services (ibid., p. 47).

7. Based on data compiled in the Freedman study. For sources see ibid., Appendix C, pp. 166–75.

8. Ibid.

9. In neither of these analyses, however, are the occupational breakdowns the same as those used in the preceding section. For example, in the census of population data used in the 1960–70 analysis, only one classification, professional-technical-kindred (PTK) is available instead of the two classifications, professional and semiprofessional-technical. In the *Current Population Survey* data utilized in the 1970–77 analysis, there are several subclassifications of PTK employment available, but they are also less useful.

10. Job increases and job decreases were computed by subtracting 1970 from 1976 employment in each industrial classification. Employment gains were designated job increases; employment losses, job decreases.

11. A careful analysis, however, would require a detailed occupational breakdown within retailing. Stock clerks and cashiers, for example, are classified as clericals not as sales workers.

12. It should be emphasized that although women have been favored "numerically," in numbers of jobs, they have not been favored in wage and salary levels.

Chapter 5

1. Although this would appear to be the most likely outcome, the reduction of transportation cost might possibly, through the lowering of prices, increase the volume of sales to the point that the richer markets may be divided among a larger

number of sellers and the distances between seller and buyer decreased. See James Hielbrun, *Urban Economics and Public Policy* (New York: St. Martin's Press, 1974), pp. 96–98.

2. Gerald Hodge, "The Prediction of Trade Center Viability in the Great Plains," *Papers of the Regional Science Association* 15 (1965): 87–115. See also Brian J. L. Berry and William Garrison, "The Functional Basis of the Central Place Hierarchy," *Economic Geography* 34 (April 1958): 145–54.

3. The coefficient is the standard deviation of employment shares in a given industry class divided by the average share of employment (all places) in that industry class.

4. Thomas M. Stanback, Jr., and Matthew Drennan, *The Transformation of the Urban Economic Base*, Special Report No. 19 (Washington, D.C.: National Commission for Manpower Policy, 1978), pp. 23–25. Classification of SMSAs is explained in Thomas M. Stanback, Jr., and Richard V. Knight, *The Metropolitan Economy* (New York: Columbia University Press, 1970), pp. 125–31.

5. The category "Mainly Business Services" shown in table 16 includes the three service categories, wholesale, FIRE, and business/repair services, plus two servicelike categories, transportation and communications. These activities are engaged to a large extent in providing for the needs of business firms. The category "Mainly Consumer Services" includes retail, recreation-entertainment, private household, medical-education, all services provided principally to consumers.

6. Robert Cohen, "The Modern Corporation and the City" (unpublished), Chapters 7 and 8.

7. Ibid., Chapter 8, pp. 11–12.

8. Jean Gottman, "Urban Centrality and the Interweaving of Quarternary Activities," *Ekistics* 29, no. 174 (May 1970): 323–25.

9. This interdependence has been extremely important in the past. In a recent study of ten major metropolitan areas, it was estimated that on average, wages and salaries of commuters accounted for 39 percent of total earnings of suburban residents in 1970. When due consideration was given to multiplier effects (that is, to local sector employment created by this purchasing power), commuter incomes accounted for, directly and indirectly, almost two-thirds of total suburban earnings. At the same time, the cities have also been dependent on the suburbs for it has been in large measure the amenities of suburban living that have made it possible for city-based activities to recruit key executives and professional personnel. See Thomas M. Stanback, Jr., and Richard V. Knight, *Suburbanization and the City* (Montclair, N.J.: Allanheld, Osmun, 1976), p. 94.

10. The Conservation of Human Resources Project, *The Corporate Headquarters Complex in New York City* (New York: The Conservation of Human Resources Project, 1977). It is interesting that there has been a recent parallel but lesser development in business services in Stamford, Connecticut, to meet certain needs of the many large headquarters in the area (Richard L. Madden, "Law Firms Expand to Serve Connecticut Business Giants," *New York Times*, March 21, 1978, p. 37).

11. Wilbur Thompson, "Economic Processes and Employment Problems in Declining Metropolitan Areas," in *Post-Industrial America: Metropolitan Decline and Interregional Job Shifts*, ed. by George Sternlieb and James W. Hughes (New Brunswick, N.J.: Center for Urban Research, 1976), p. 192.

116

Chapter 6

1. Daniel Bell, *The Coming of Post Industrial Society* (New York: Basic Books, Inc., 1976), p. ix.
2. Ibid., p. 14.
3. Ibid., p. 128.
4. Ibid., pp. 154–55.
5. Ibid., pp. 136, 146.
6. "The Office of the Future," *Business Week*, June 30, 1975, p. 49.
7. Ibid.
8. J. Christopher Burns, "The Evolution of Office Information Systems," *Datamation*, April 1977, p. 62.
9. Ibid.
10. Ibid.
11. "The Office of the Future," p. 50.
12. Ibid.
13. Ibid.
14. Thomas E. Mullaney, "Tax Fever Spreads," *New York Times*, July 9, 1978, p. F15.
15. It has been objected, however, that the state deficits amounted to no more than $6–8 billion after adjustment for the impact of state pension plans (ibid.).
16. Victor R. Fuchs, "The Growing Importance of the Service Industries," *Journal of Business of the University of Chicago* 38 (October 1965): 360–62.
17. Fuchs, "Service Industries," p. 369.

Appendix

1. In discussing the AID procedure, Freedman states: "The essence of AID is sequential one-way analysis of variance that partitions the data into a series of mutually exclusive subgroups. The criterion for each division is that level of the predictor that most reduces the variance of the dependent variables, mean annual earnings. At each stage, subgroups are treated separately in the same fashion and further subdivided. AID itself determines the final number of groups. It specifies the interactions of the independent variables and thus permits observations of different causal structures in the various subgroups of the data" *(Labor Markets: Segments and Shelters* [Montclair, N.J.: Allanheld, Osmun, 1976], p. 17).

Index

A

Advanced corporate services, 85–88; in accounting, 87–88; banking and, 86–87; and central cities, 92; and corporate headquarters, 86, 91–92; legal, 87; and market size, 20–22

Agglomeration, 77, 81, 83

B

Baumol, William, 30, 42

Bell, Daniel, 98–100, 106

Business services. *See* Producer services

C

Central business district, 89

Central city, 89–91; female employment opportunities in, 92; revitalization of, 92–93, 96

Central place theory. *See* Location of services

Coefficients of variation, 79, 80 (*table*), 116 n. 3

Cohen, Robert, 19–20, 86–88

Complementarities of demand. *See* Demand. complementarities of, between goods and services

Computers. *See* Technology

Consumer demand: aggregate growth of, 15–16; for business services, 21; and government expenditures, 84; growth of, for durable goods compared to services, 8–9, 13, 16; growth of, for services, 7–9, 10, 12–16, 27

Consumer services: costs of, 12–13; employment growth in, in SMSAs, 84–85; growth of, in suburbs, 89; quality of, 13; variety of, 15–16. *See also* Consumer demand

Corporate headquarters, 86, 90–92, 94, 107

D

Demand, complementarities of, between goods and services: and consumers, 8, 10, 16, 99; and effects of productivity differentials on relative prices, 37–38, 41–42, 108; and growth of service employment, 108–9; linkages from, 2, 41, 97; and not-for-profit sector, 99; and private sector output and public sector services, 25; and problems of measurement of service productivity, 41; and producers, 21–22

119

E

Earnings, 45–51, 57; and labor market segments, 111–12; of non-whites in services, 56–57; of women in services, 54–55, 57, 71; of young workers in services, 56–57. *See also* Sheltering in service employment

Economies of scale, 18, 71

Employment: changes, 1960–1970, 62–65; changes, 1970–1977, 66–68; industry shares of, among SMSAs, 79; occupational and skill mix of, 44–45, 85; occupational distribution of, between services and nonservices, 45–48. *See also* Employment growth in services; Employment in services

Employment growth in services, 4, 62–71, 82, 84–85, 89, 91, 95–96, 99–100, 107–9; in business services, by type of SMSA, 82, 96; compared to nonservices, 68–69; in local sector services, 89, 96; in "low-end" service jobs, 99–100; and new technology, 102, 106; occupational composition of, 63, 65, 67–68, 70, 84, 93–94, 100; and public sector services, 103; and servicelike work, 68–69; and small firms, 103–4

Employment in services, 44–72; as major source of growth in jobs, 4, 6, 29, 62–71; distribution of occupations and earnings in, 45–48, 106; female, 53–55, 57; and industrial groupings, 67–68, 84–85; industry shares of, among SMSAs, 79; occupational composition of, 63–65, 67–68, 71, 84–85; part-time, 48–49; sheltering in, 49–52; upward mobility and, 107. *See also* Employment growth in services

Equity, 107

Export activity, 78–79; services as, 95

Export sector: nature of, and recreational and cultural institutions, 81; services, 4–5, 96

External economies, 77

F

Female: employment and earnings in services, 4, 53–54, 55, 57; employment growth in services, 4, 62–65, 67, 71; employment in central city, 92; employment, upgrading of, 4, 67, 98, 115 n. 12; importance in service work force, 99; young workers, 56

Freedman, Marcia, 114–15 n. 1, 110–12

Fuchs, Victor, 3, 36, 103, 106

G

Ginzberg, Eli, 22–26

Goods sector of the economy: definition and characteristics of, 5–6; employment change in, 95–96; increasing consumption in, 12–13; and public needs, 26; wages in, 30. *See also* Demand, complementarities of, between goods and services; Nonservice sector of the economy

Gottman, Jean, 90

Greenfield, Harry I., 18, 111

Guiliano, Vincent E., 101–2

H

Hierarchy of cities, 74–75, 98; and export services, 95; and occupational distribution, 93–94; and specialization of business services, 88

Housing, 90, 92–93

I

Income growth, 12–14; and local sector services, 96; and service employment, 108

Library of Congress Cataloging in Publication Data

Stanback, Thomas M.
  Understanding the service economy.

  (Policy studies in employment and welfare; no. 35)
  "Prepared under contract no. USDL 21-36-76-18 from the Employment and
Training Administration, U.S. Department of Labor."
  Includes bibliographical references and index.
  1. Service industries—United States   2. Service industries workers—
United States.   3. Municipal services—United States.   I. Title.
HD9981.5.S7   338.4'0973   79-2372
ISBN 0–8018–2249–1